SOUND HEALTH

SOUND HEALTH

The Music and Sounds That Make Us Whole

Steven Halpern, Ph.D.,
with Louis Savary, Ph.D.

Harper & Row, Publishers, San Francisco

New York, Grand Rapids, Philadelphia, St. Louis

1817   *London, Singapore, Sydney, Tokyo, Toronto*

FIRST EDITION

Designer: Jim Mennick

Library of Congress Cataloging in Publication Data

Halpern, Steven.
    SOUND HEALTH.

    1. Health. 2. Sound—Physiological aspects. 3. Sound—Psychological aspects.
4. Music—Physiological aspects. 5. Music—Psychological aspects. I. Savary,
Louis M. II. Title.
RA776.5.H254   1985   613   84-48219
ISBN 0-06-063671-8

89   10   9   8   7   6

CONTENTS

INTRODUCTION

The ultimate purpose of this book is to foster health, peace, and harmony in your life and in the world.

Our planet pulses with life and energy. The responsibility for its physical health, its emotional sanity, and its spiritual creativity has been placed in our human hands. As our planet moves in its evolutionary trajectory through time, we humans sit at the controls. Yes, each one of us.

This is the discovery of our decade: the future of life on earth is up to us. In years past, many people had given over such responsibility entirely to physicians, pharmacists, friends, family, even to the authoritative announcer's voice they heard selling medical and health aids. Today, however, people have confidently reassumed their personal right to be in charge of their own health. As more and more people consciously awaken to this way of living, realizing that "you do not have to be sick in order to get better," they begin to assume responsibility for the foods and medicines they consume.

Interest in health maintenance and preventive medicine has become a phenomenon of unprecedented growth. People today are learning to use the tools of health to foster their own wholeness. In a quiet revolution, humanity is awakening to its right to be healthy.

But one element in human health is often overlooked: "sound" health. Sound—whether it be the music of instruments, the voice of a singer, the hum of human conversation, the ringing of a telephone, or the tolling of a church bell—can be a powerful ingredient in the formula of health.

In this book, we share some of the ways we have found to use sound and music to help keep humans well. We place the tools for sound health in your hands—because, like many others in our new age of self-responsibility and consciousness, we have become aware that the tools for sound health, like the tools for all human health, belong to everyone.

Sound is a powerful force that may be used to help bring about health, peace, and harmony. We hope that through this book you will come to realize that you can be a sound force in the world.

As we become more aware of sound, culturally as well as individually, we will begin to look at the world in sound terms as well as visual ones. A landscape is usually defined in terms of objects that are seen. Now we must also learn to hear a soundscape, that is, to define our surroundings in terms of the events heard.

If it is true that you are what you eat, it may just as accurately be said that you are what you listen to.

In the past few decades, sound pollution—invisible, odorless, and tasteless—has grown to epidemic proportions. Avoiding noise is no longer merely a personal problem, such as getting a neighbor to lower the volume on a blasting stereo. Sound pollution has become a social disease. Vast quantities of unwelcome sound, from jet planes to jackhammers, are daily imposed on almost everyone.

As individuals and as a society, we can do more than simply to lament the loss of quiet or to complain against irritating noise. There are alternatives. We can create the kind of sound we want.

It is our purpose in this book not only to raise awareness of the harmful sounds that we tolerate, wittingly or unwittingly, in our environment, but also to present a variety of ways to use relaxing and healing sounds. Beside reducing our intake of socially imposed noise, we believe that a healthy diet of sound and music is available to help relax and restore us and to put us in harmony with ourselves and nature.

We are deeply indebted to those scientists who have begun to research the effects of sound on the human body and mind. We have conducted some sound research ourselves and are eager to do more. We hope that the questions our book raises will stimulate others to explore new issues in this pioneering field.

For much of the information, insights, stories, and suggestions in this book, we are grateful to the many people who have reported to us what proved to be helpful or harmful in their sound diet. We welcome this wisdom and experience from people who have accepted responsibility for their own sound health.

Remember: You can begin to do things to enhance your sound environment right now. It takes no special training or equipment. You already have all you need: your own human instrument.

ACKNOWLEDGMENTS

This book is a result of the influence of many levels of input. Among the many, too numerous to mention specifically, several stand out.

To Jack Clarke and Al Glover, who helped me hear—and play—my own song. To Itzhak "Ben" Bentov, whose personal and professional contact helped turn me on to a paradigm for understanding the "tunable" nature of our human instrument. To Manfred Clynes, Ph.D., who has proven what I intuited about the existence of musical archetypes, and has discovered and mapped a whole new science of music and communication. To John Diamond, M.D., who has done so much to help awaken and educate people to the true nature, purpose, and power of music. Many thanks to Dan Kientz and Stanley Krippner, who helped me set up and run my own experiments to measure the relationship between music and relaxation. Heartfelt appreciation to David Porter and Roger Wiersema at the Music Annex Recording Studio for helping me get the music that I hear inside my head recorded onto tape.

To Carl Trondhjem and Victoria Gindele, who so effectively handle the day-to-day administration of the business known as Halpern Sounds, and who liberated me to devote myself to my music and to my writing. To Ed West, for his assistance in handling my personal appearances, and mid-wifing the development of the "Soundwave 2000" series.

Very special thanks to Lou Savary, who courageously tackled thousands of pages of rough manuscript, and conscientiously cut, organized, and clarified the material. And finally, many thanks to

Glenn Setty, who patiently transcribed hundreds of hours of dictation and who is responsible for typing and retyping this manuscript.

STEVEN HALPERN

Belmont, California

PART ONE

Sound Body

Chapter 1

SOUND AWARENESS

Nutrition Awareness

For the first time in human history, a great number of people have become nutritionally conscious. Many were brought to a new level of health awareness by pioneering books, such as Adelle Davis's *Let's Get Healthy* and *Let's Eat Right to Get Fit*. They began to assume responsibility for the foods they ate and how they felt afterwards.

This increase in nutritional awareness provided the impetus for health food centers and grocery stores to offer produce that was unprocessed or naturally and organically grown. As a result, many commercial food producers now make available an alternative line of natural foods, without artificial flavors and preservatives, without excess sodium, and with low cholesterol levels.

Today, people who care about good nutrition can eat more consciously and healthfully than they could a decade ago. They have choices and alternatives. They can open their mouths to what is nutritious and close their mouths to what is not.

Sound Consciousness

The time has come for us to become conscious of healthy and unhealthy sounds, and to assume responsibility for the sounds we take into our bodies.

Sound awareness is especially important, for although we can easily close our mouths and eyes to what we don't want to take in, we can't really close our ears. Nature did not give us earlids. Our ears remain open and working even while we sleep.

The fact is that we humans are ingesting and digesting sound in one form or another twenty-four hours a day.

Just as we can undermine our health by habitually consuming certain foods over extended periods, we can also undermine our health by consuming certain sounds and noises over extended periods.

On the other hand, just as certain foods and nutritional supplements taken on a regular basis can increase our vitality and general health, so a regular diet of certain kinds of music and sounds can help our bodies and minds to achieve a higher level of health.

It is of primary concern that we become aware of the power of sound in our lives, and that we begin taking more responsibility for the sounds in our environment.

Dr. John Knowles, former president of the Rockefeller Foundation, reported in the *A.R.E. Medical Clinic Newsletter* said, "The next great leap in the health care of the American people will be when the people learn to take care of themselves." You *can* begin to take care of yourself as far as sounds are concerned. You can lessen the negative effects of noise in your life, and you can begin to evoke the positive potentials of music and sound for greater health and happiness.

Choosing Healthy Sound

Properly chosen sounds can actually help bring you into a greater degree of physical and psychological harmony and balance.

Perhaps the most important element in choosing healthy sound is knowing what feels right and works for you. Of course, what is music to your ears may be annoying to a neighbor, or even to another family member. Like taste in food, taste in sound differs with individuals.

You will have to test your own sensations and responses to different kinds of aural "food," to learn which sounds tend to nourish you. But first of all, you will have to become aware of the sounds you are already taking into yourself.

An Exercise in Sound Awareness

What are the sounds that you listen to each day? Are they welcome or unwelcome?

In order to focus consciously on the sounds that your body is ingesting, sit quietly for at least five minutes and make a list of each different sound that you hear. Next to each sound on your list put a "W" (for a welcome sound) or a "U" (for an unwelcome sound). You'll be surprised by what you discover.

In a five-minute period one young man listed only one sound he enjoyed—music on his personal stereo. The rest he found annoying: the roar of a motorcycle, refrigerator hum, the buzz of the air conditioner, the rumble of a passing truck, squeaky floorboards in the apartment above, a telephone ringing, and neighbors talking.

Sound-Sensitive People

Some people are more sensitive to sound than others. For example, one man told me that when he was a child playing on the street, the noise of a passing truck would so irritate him he would have to cover his ears with his hands, while his playmates never seemed to be bothered by the sound.

Just as some people are highly taste-sensitive and can differentiate between very subtle flavors, so sound-sensitive people react very strongly to sounds, especially unwelcome ones. Sounds are clearly felt in their bodies. Harsh sounds are capable of giving them a headache or an upset stomach, while certain pleasant sounds have the ability to calm or energize them. Some music can even send them into a state of rapture.

We have found many sound-sensitives in our workshops. These people are deeply relieved to discover that they are not alone in the world, and that they no longer have to feel ostracized or "different" because of their sensitivity to sound.

Many of these people had carried a stigma throughout their lives—a sense that they were not normal, that there was something the matter with them because of their sensitivity to sound. For those of you who are sound-sensitive and may have felt this way, be assured that you are quite normal and healthy.

Awareness through Sound Research

Certain kinds of foods that delight us—such as sugar, caffeine, alcohol, and chocolate—may prove to be unhealthy for our bodies. Similarly, certain rhythms and sounds, even though we seem to enjoy them, may prove to be unhealthy for our bodies. It is important to become aware of these harmful and unhealthy sounds. Sound researchers can show us ways to develop such awareness.

On the basis of research in the field of behavioral kinesiology, psychiatrist John Diamond reports in his book *Your Body Doesn't Lie* that the relative strength of our physical muscles can be measured while we listen to different musical selections. Through testing, it can be shown that certain selections either strengthen or weaken the muscles of a particular individual.

In his book, Dr. Diamond describes some simple tests you can use to determine whether or not a certain musical selection is healthy for you.

Just as no amount of persuasion can ever convince our blood vessels that plenty of salt is good for them, so neither can we convince our bodies that certain noxious sounds are good for them. Regardless of what your mind thinks of a particular sound or piece of music, your body has its own reality and response to it.

Contemporary sound researchers are letting the body speak for itself. They are measuring its response through muscle testing, biofeedback, electro-acupuncture, and the like. Our bodies and organs seem to know instinctively the sounds that make them healthy. Given a choice, our bodies tend to choose life-enhancing music and sounds.

Entire Body Responsive to Sound

Although the ear is still given credit as the major pathway for aural processing, there is a great deal of evidence that the entire body is sensitive to sound. All the cells in our bodies have vibratory properties and hence are capable of being sound receptors. Since these effects often occur below the threshold of conscious awareness, they can occur even when the mind is not consciously processing the incoming information. For example, even while we sleep, whether or not we are conscious of the continuous rumble of traffic outside, our body hears it and reacts to it.

Moreover, certain unnoticed sounds can have a pronounced effect on us down to the very marrow of our bones. When vibrations below the auditory threshold are distributed universally in our environment—such as the network of ordinary 60-cycle alternating current that flows through the electrical wiring in our homes and offices—they may even affect the body's own natural pulse and pitch.

Sound at the Center of Our Being

Sound researcher and music professor R. Murray Schafer discovered that today's American and Canadian students find that the easiest pitch to retain and recall spontaneously corresponds to the music note B natural. During meditation, after becoming deeply relaxed, students were asked to sing whatever tone seemed to arise naturally from the center of their being. B natural was more frequently the response than any other tone. Students in Germany and other European countries, however, given the same situation and instructions, tended to hum G sharp.

What accounts for the difference? Schafer points out that in America and Canada, electricity operates on an alternating current of 60 cycles per second. We hear this frequency subconsciously in the activity of all electrical devices, including lights, amplifiers, motors, generators, and appliances. We are literally surrounded by vibrations of 60 cycles per second. The resonant frequency of 60-

cycle electrical current relates to the B natural tone on a musical scale.

On the other hand, in Europe the alternating electrical current is 50 cycles per second, which relates musically to G sharp!

Thus, the sound that seems to come from the deepest part of our being is probably produced by the continual intake, year after year, of the electrical current's resonant frequency one hears in virtually all our homes and buildings. As individuals, this means that, as a result of unconscious conditioning at the cellular level, our bodies ingest and are transformed by sounds and vibrations to which we rarely give a second thought.

Levels of Awareness

We often fail to realize that while the mind can condition itself to ignore noxious sounds, the body cannot. The physical organism goes on responding to the ocean of vibrations in which we live, often in ways that may contribute to a general feeling of stress and tension, even though we are unaware of the source of that feeling.

Ours is a visually oriented society. We are more likely to be aware of what we see than of what we hear. We don't tend to notice sounds unless they startle or annoy us, so we tend to take for granted, ignore, or deny many of the sounds of our environment.

New Awarenesses

While many today unquestioningly consume whatever noise, sounds and music are being fed to them by the sound producers, others are beginning to ask questions. A new trend of sound health inquiry is starting, one that will ultimately make all of us conscious and concerned about the ways in which we nourish our bodies with sound.

Many people today are aware that it is now possible to satisfy our sound needs in ways that were not possible ten years ago. The science of sound health has come a long way.

On the one hand, researchers are discovering how *certain kinds of music and sounds may contribute to stress, tension, headache, nausea, hearing loss, disturbed sleep, poor digestion, irritability, lack of concentration, and hyperactivity.* On the other hand, people are listening to—and composing—music to enhance their health and life. They are learning how to choose and create music to *facilitate such things as relaxation, concentration, learning, creativity, meditation, muscle response, digestion, mood change, psychotherapy, and self-healing.*

With the growth of sound awareness focused on health, we now have the opportunity to begin paying attention to sound as it affects our total health. In taking care of our own sound health, we may experience new vistas of self-discovery and aliveness that we never knew existed.

Chapter 2

SOUND POLLUTION

The Abuse of Music

"In trying to track a suspected Soviet submarine last month," began a recent report in the *New York Times* (Nov. 16, 1982), "the Swedish Navy had difficulty finding sailors who could hear well enough to operate the listening devices. The hearing of vast numbers of young people, a Navy captain said, apparently has been permanently damaged by years of listening to rock music."

Abusive noise among the young is a worldwide problem. Dr. David Lipscomb of the noise laboratory at the University of Tennessee recently found that more than 60 percent of the incoming college freshmen he tested had significant hearing loss in the high-frequency range. He suspects that this exposure to harmful noise is on the increase; only a year before, a similar hearing test revealed only 30 percent of incoming freshmen had significant hearing loss.

The same *New York Times* article cited a 1982 Japanese survey that discovered unexplained hearing difficulties in a number of young people, many of whom reported listening to stereo headsets for more than twenty-four hours a week.

Dr. Lipscomb commented on this awesome trend in hearing loss among young people in *Science Year: The World Book Science Annual, 1982*. He wrote "Some had hearing no better than that of men between the ages of 60 and 69. In effect, these young people were entering their working life with retirement-age ears."

In the Concert Hall

While the loud music of young people can be damaging, lovers of classical music should not be lulled into security. Two Swedish researchers, Alf Axelsson and Fredrik Lindgren, report in a Swedish magazine *Working Environment* (1982) that even listening to Beethoven can do damage.

Employed by the Department of Audiology and Occupational Medicine at Sahlgrenska Hospital in Gothenburg, the pair of researchers found that 59 of the 139 orchestral musicians they studied exhibited worse than average hearing losses. The volume of orchestral music in the concert hall often exceeded 85 decibels, Sweden's legal eight-hour workplace exposure limit. Although concert-goers were subjected to these volumes for only a few hours and at some distance from the orchestra, the musicians themselves were immersed in the sounds for about forty hours each week. Trombone and French horn players showed the greatest high-frequency hearing loss. Similar research, with similar results, was carried out with members of the Zurich Symphony Orchestra.

Sound and Noise

Sound is produced when something vibrates, either randomly or in a periodically repeated motion. Noise is a specific category of sound, generally described as unwanted sound.

Sounds are graded according to their decibel level. Decibels (dB), named in honor of Alexander Graham Bell, are the units of measurement for the pressure a sound creates.

The sound level meter is the basic instrument used to measure the physical characteristics of sound. The higher the decibel level, the louder the sound. One decibel, or 1 dBA, is the quietest sound the average person can hear.*

Rising Ambient Noise

When Mozart was composing at the end of the eighteenth century, the city of Vienna was so quiet that fire alarms could be given

---

* The A in dBA indicates that the decibel meter being used is of the A (humanly audible) type. This means it is adapted to the biases of the human ear against low-frequency sounds. Thus a certain dBA indicates a decibel level *as people perceive it*.

verbally, by a shouting watchman mounted on top of St. Stefan's Cathedral.

As recently as just before World War II, the brass bell on top of a fire truck was loud enough to clear traffic from its path.

By the 1950s, however, the bell was no longer sufficiently loud to rise above the ambient noise and the siren came into common use. In 1964 the ambient noise level on the streets in England was loud enough to require a siren's volume to reach 88 dBA at 50 feet under calm conditions.

The current noise level in large U.S. cities requires police cars to use a yelping siren that measures 122 dBA. At 120 dBA—which jet engines, rock bands, discos, firecrackers, sirens, and personal stereos can register—noise reaches the threshold of pain.

Thus our ears and bodies are enduring more decibels than ever before in history. City dwellers suffer the worst assaults. They must tolerate street noise, road repairs, construction vehicles, subway trains, car horns, police and fire sirens, loud music, and airplanes.

But the suburbs and the country are not noise-free: farm equipment, highway noise, lawn mowers, dishwashers, and vacuum cleaners all present problems. The introduction of snowmobiles, for instance, has made deafness and ear disease the largest public health problem in the Canadian arctic.

The American Speech and Hearing Association estimates that 40 million Americans daily live, work, or play around noise that is dangerously loud. In light of these conditions, there are three important sound facts to remember.

Three Facts of Sound Health

First, *the ill effects of noise are cumulative.* Therefore keep exposure time around unwanted noise to a minimum. Strong vibrations from excessive noise actually wear out the sensory cells of the ear until they can no longer respond. Hearing impairment is hard to recognize, since it is painless and develops slowly. If you are exposed to sounds in the upper-decibel range for long periods of time, sooner or later your hearing may be harmed. Unfortunately, most people don't notice hearing impairment until it becomes advanced and interferes with communication.

Second, *noise-induced hearing impairment is permanent*. With special training, a hearing aid may help some people hear and communicate a little better, but it can't bring back what is already damaged or destroyed. Medicine or surgery will not cure noise-induced hearing impairment.

Third, *decibels increase their effect logarithmically*. Decibels are not linear units like miles or pounds, rather, they mark points on a sharply rising curve of volume or intensity. Canadian sound researcher and composer R. Murray Schafer in his book *The Tuning of the World* claims that a rise of 3 dBA is equivalent to a doubling of sound energy. Other researchers say that with every 10-dBA rise in the meter, people near the sound perceive its loudness by another multiple of ten.

Thus, while 10 dBA is ten times greater in intensity than 1 dBA, 20 dBA is ten times greater in intensity than 10 dBA, 20 dBA is one hundred times greater than 1 dBA, 30 dBA is one thousand times greater than 1 dBA, and so on. At this rate, sound registering 100 dBA on the meter is 1 billion times as intense as 1 dBA.

Professor of audiology at New York University and consultant at New York City Department of Health Maurice H. Miller, writing in the *New York University Education Quarterly* (1978), gives the following example of sound's logarithmic effect. "While 90 dBA is equal to the sound of a train roaring into a subway station, 100 dBA equals the sound of 10 trains pulling into the station simultaneously, and 110 dBA represents 100 trains."

In practical terms, this means that if we can safely tolerate eight consecutive hours of noise at 90 dBA without hearing impairment, we cannot tolerate more than fifteen consecutive *minutes* at 115 dBA!

The following is a list of noise makers and their corresponding decibel levels, compiled from various publications of the U.S. Environmental Protection Agency:

Sound	Decibel Level
faucet dripping	40
refrigerator	45
moderate rainfall	50
chirping birds	60
washing machine	65
vacuum cleaner	70–75
kitchen mixer	70
cocktail party (100 guests)	70–85
busy traffic	75–85
window air conditioner	80
alarm clock	80
diesel truck	80
electric shaver (at close range)	85
screaming child	90–115
jackhammer	100
chain saw	100
subway train (inside)	100
motorcycles	100
power motor	100–105
live rock music (amplified)	90–130
hockey game crowd	120
loud thunder	120
air raid siren	130
jet engine (at take off)	120–140

In the past, people considered noise only a nuisance. Today we recognize that it can be dangerous.

According to William H. Stewart, former U.S. Surgeon General, in *Science News*, June 1982, "Calling noise a nuisance is like calling smog an inconvenience. Noise must be considered a hazard to the health of people everywhere."

The Unfriendly Skies

We have become so accustomed to painful noises that the Environmental Protection Agency (EPA) defines a tolerable level of noise as one where two people indoors standing one foot apart can converse without having to shout!

In many American homes, people seated at their own dining room table cannot converse without shouting while a jet plane passes overhead. This situation is common to many who live in big cities.

A government study of jet noise published in August 1980 estimated that 100,000 people living near airports will get almost no noise abatement for at least the next twenty years, and suggests that such families should eventually be relocated in quieter neighborhoods.

That study (*Aviation Noise: The Next Twenty Years*, prepared by the EPA at the direction of Congress) also recommends that the government plan to soundproof the homes of an additional 2.5 million people near airports who are expected still to be suffering from high jet noise levels two decades from now, *even after airlines and airports meet federal noise abatement standards.*

That's extraordinary! The ultimate solution to the jet noise problem, as the federal government sees it, is to learn to live with it. Some people must move, and others must soundproof their homes. What about the jet planes, the source of the noise?

Dr. John Schettino, then Director of Noise Abatement Technology at the EPA, said that the biggest problems include the inertia of airlines that put off replacing noisy planes; the inertia of aircraft manufacturers that drag their feet in developing quieter engines; and, most important, the inertia of communities that refuse to use restrictive zoning to prevent housing construction near airports.

Noise at Home

Once upon a time people could say, "My home is my castle—a place of refuge, a retreat from the world, an oasis of peace and quiet." But no longer. Even in our own homes today, our bodies are constantly assaulted by a non-stop barrage of sonic stimuli.

The blender, the electric can opener, the vacuum cleaner—all can cause sound-sensitive people to feel pain. Many household noises can reach such loud volumes that you cannot hear the voices of others even in the same room. When you can't hear without shouting, chances are the decibel level is unhealthful and excessive.

Machines in the home are designed to make our lives easier. But long periods of use coupled with exposure to other elements of the sound environment can combine to damage our sensory neural hearing mechanism. A University of Wisconsin study showed that noises produced by common household items—electric shavers, food processors, vent fans, garbage disposals, electric mixers, knife sharpeners, dishwashers, vacuum cleaners—produced a state of heightened body arousal and general nervous tension.

Dr. Jack C. Westman, a Wisconsin psychiatrist, believes that home noise contributes to noise-related health damage and to conflicts between family members.

According to the EPA booklet *Noise Around Our Home* (1980), nearly half of all Americans are regularly exposed to levels of noise that interfere with such important natural activities as speaking, listening, or performing tasks.

Unnecessary Noise

Much household noise is technologically unnecessary. Two common perpetrators of unnecessary noise are the dishwasher and the vacuum cleaner. Both devices can be made to work much more quietly. The problem is that many housekeepers don't believe that these appliances are working properly unless they make noise.

According to Dr. Maurice H. Miller, "Curiously, when manufacturers, goaded by the Environmental Protection Agency and vocal consumer groups, develop appliances that are quieter than preceding models, American consumers tend not to purchase them, for we have conditioned ourselves to equate noise with efficiency. One manufacturer designed a quieter vacuum cleaner about five years ago which was consistently rejected by consumers."

The basic selling principle here is that if an appliance makes noise, it's working. Thus, by their reasoning, noise is good.

We now know better.

Noise Affects the Sleep of Babies and Adults

High levels of noise in the home, from television sets, radios, and other sources, were shown to disrupt the sensory and motor skills of children during the first two years of life.

Research psychologist Dr. Theodore D. Wacks at Purdue University, reported in *The New York Times*, Nov. 16, 1982, believes that noise stress prompts babies to retreat into their own inner space. His research found that babies living in noisy homes were slower to imitate adult behavior and persisted in infantile habits longer than babies in quieter homes. Noise also delayed verbal development and exploratory activity.

Studies at Stanford University attempting to measure how noise affects sleep found that even when people don't think noise has affected them while sleeping, their energy level and efficiency at work the following day are markedly reduced. Similarly, in 1983, French researchers Muzet and Ehrhart at the Bioclimatic Study Center found that even though test subjects no longer reported being disturbed by noises during sleep, their bodies failed to habituate to the noise. Muzet and Ehrhart also demonstrated that the long-term effects on the cardiovascular system of low noise during sleep are much greater than had been hypothesized.

What You Can Do

There are many simple steps that you can take to help yourself to sound health:

- To reduce noise, you can put foam pads under blenders, mixers, food processors, typewriters, and the like.
- You can use sound insulation and vibration mounts when installing dishwashers, clothes washers, refrigerators, and so on.
- Before buying new appliances, you can compare the noisiness of different models, and select those that are quieter.
- Be especially careful when purchasing children's toys that make loud and sharp sounds. Some explosive-type sounds can cause permanent injury to young ears.

- When you are looking for your next home or apartment, take into account sound factors such as airport noise, traffic noise, and noise leakage from neighbors' homes or apartments, especially at common walls.

You can add extra insulation to your home for sound efficiency as well as energy efficiency. The same insulation that you install to keep your living space warmer in winter and cooler in summer also helps to cut down on sound pollution intruding from the outside. Storm windows, for example, significantly diminish unwanted outdoor sounds such as barking dogs and traffic.

Sound insulation is also part of a "good neighbor policy." It can help contain the sounds that you make inside your home, whether listening to your stereo or practicing the piano, from leaking into the world outside your home.

Carpeting, rugs, and draperies absorb sounds while preventing heat loss. Because these items are not permanent additions to the structure of the dwelling, you can take them with you when you move.

Peace of Mind—What's It Worth?

Consider, if you will, that the $500 you might spend for rugs and insulation is worth much more to you in terms of peace of mind and improved health. Noise control in the home may indirectly cut down on your doctor bills. Less incoming noise means less stress and enhanced resistance to disease. It also means less dependence on stimulating drugs, such as caffeine, or on relaxing drugs, such as alcohol, to deal with the fatigue or stress that is often a result of noise.

A Harmonious Home

Despite outside noise, you can create and control the sound in your own living space in ways that support and nourish you. There are many other simple measures that you can take. One antidote to sound pollution in your own life is to surround yourself with music that you find useful and harmonious. (This topic will be treated at greater length in the chapters called Sound Relaxation and Sound

Diet.) One way to create a sound atmosphere is to assemble your own personal library of beautiful, relaxing music.

Sound Inventory

Take a sound inventory of the different sound makers in your home. As you make your list, note whether the sounds are welcome or unwelcome.

Have each member of your household take a similar sound inventory. Then discuss your findings with each other.

Three Important Signals

When it comes to protecting your ears from the damaging effects of noise-induced hearing loss, *prevention* is the key word. Audiologists suggest three specific signals to watch out for as a precaution against possible hearing loss.

First, *if you have to shout* directly into another person's ear in order to be able to talk in the presence of loud sound, there is great risk that such sound can cause hearing loss.

Second, *if your ears ring* after leaving a noisy area, you have been exposed to dangerous sound levels.

Third, *if you experience dullness of hearing* after being exposed to high-level sounds, your hearing sensitivity has probably been diminished. This effect, a shift in the hearing threshold, is usually temporary, and normal hearing should return.

Constant repetition of situations that produce any of these signs can produce permanent hearing damage.

Precaution is Up to You

According to the EPA, the maximum sound intensity to which most adults can be exposed for eight hours a day without any risk of hearing loss is 75 dBA. And yet, the Occupational Safety and Health Administration (OSHA) has estimated that more than half of American production workers are exposed to continual workplace noise of 80 decibels or higher.

OSHA's Hearing Conservation Amendment is designed to protect the rights of industrial workers; but it does nothing to protect the sound rights of farm workers and workers at construction sites, nor does it protect office workers.

Everyone who works in an office—secretaries, clerical workers, managers, and executives—must face the stressful effects of office lighting, computer radiation, poor acoustics, the noise of other voices, machinery, traffic, and telephones, all of which make it difficult to pay attention, to be heard and to converse.

It is interesting to consider that current federal policy has shifted the responsibility from federal to state and local control. In many cases, the issues of occupational health and safety are no longer concerned with how much the problems are hurting workers, but rather how much the solutions are hurting corporate profits.

In San Francisco, California, the recent victory of nonsmokers in claiming their rights to a smoke-free workplace is a good example of people taking responsibility for their own health. Workers should similarly be able to demand a noise-free workplace.

We have the technology to decrease the amount of noise that machinery and vehicles make. Once we get our priorities straight, there's no question that more appropriate and healthful levels of sound and noise will be available to the mutual enhancement of both corporate profits and personal health.

The introduction of quiet, new equipment would give a new reality to the term "silent" business partner. As offices become more healthy and more humane, they will also become more efficient.

Several cities in the country, among them Bloomington, Minnesota, and San Diego, California, have set up exemplary noise control programs that have resulted in a greatly enhanced community consciousness of noise and a greatly enhanced sound quality of living. These are wonderful models for other cities to follow. Communities that would like to start noise control programs can contact these cities directly, or get some help from the EPA's Community Network Program. In addition, in the late 1970s, the federal government initiated the Quiet Community program. If you are interested, we recommend contacting the EPA for current status and information.

The successful story of San Diego's attempt to control noise is told in the two-hundred page EPA publication *San Diego, California: A Case History of a Municipal Noise Control Program.* See the section on Sound Helps for the address.

It is quite possible that your city or state already has noise abatement laws or ordinances. But it is one thing for a city to have noise abatement laws on the books, and another matter to have that legislation enforced. Share this information with your neighbors and friends. In unity there is strength, and in strength there is the prospect of a healthy environment for us all.

Standing Up For Your Own Rights

We do not simply have to put up with noise. Indeed, by putting up with it we are silently agreeing with it and indirectly supporting it. There are other alternatives.

The worldwide noise problem was serious enough to warrant a statement form UNESCO. In 1969 the General Assembly of the International Music Council of UNESCO in Paris denounced the abusive use of background music in public and private places.

There are many ways that you as an individual can take a stand for your own sound rights. One of the simplest is to be aware of the noise level of your surroundings. If it is excessively high, take your patronage elsewhere—and let the owner know the reason.

For example: if you enter a restaurant that sounds more like a football stadium on Sunday afternoon, chances are (a) you won't be able to have a fruitful business or romantic conversation, and (b) your body won't be able to properly digest the food that you eat, due to the inhibiting effect of noise on the secretion of gastric juices.

What do you do when "noise is on the menu?" Before you leave, you may consider asking the restaurant manager to lower the volume of the music or to change the style of the music to something more conducive to dining. Another alternative is to ask for "no noise" sections in restaurants, much as we have "no smoking" sections.

Music at Fitness Centers

The pop-sound culture has invaded not only our homes and restaurants, but fitness centers as well. The problem is that the music people are using to exercise with or dance to often employs the stopped-anapestic rhythms that have actually been shown to weaken the strength of the muscles. Such music throws off muscular coordination and confuses the brain. The net result is that it will be even harder for you to learn tricky aerobics movements because the music itself may be confusing.

As an experiment, notice what happens when you work out in silence or to music other than heavy rock or disco.

Equally offensive to many health and fitness seekers is the fact that the music at these facilities often comes out of the speakers in a distorted fashion because it is played too loud. This further weakens the body, and the volume makes it difficult to follow the instructions of the instructor. When bass frequencies are boosted to simulate a disco on Friday night, the sound becomes "muddy" and produces a further assault on the body.

In short, studies have shown that fast, loud music with a booming bass is not the most conducive music to a healthy workout. We think that you owe it to yourself to try some sound alternatives.

Stereo Headsets

Although you can generate a lot of volume with ordinary floor-model loudspeakers connected to a home stereo system, other family members or neighbors will usually complain as soon as its volume gets annoyingly loud. Personal headphones offer an attractive alternative. Not only do they provide listening that is private and undisturbing to others, but they make music come alive for the listener in ways most floor speakers could never do.

For this reason they pose a distinct danger. Because they direct sound into the ear so totally and efficiently, it is possible to subject yourself to dangerously intense sound without realizing it.

How can you tell when the volume is at a dangerously high level? Use the three important signals mentioned above as a warning. If you are unable to converse with someone nearby while the headset is on, or if you experience ringing in the ears or dullness of hearing after you remove the headset, the volume level is dangerously loud for your ears.

Quiet Noise

There is growing evidence that noise need not be loud to be troublesome.

One such common sound is the low rumble of the refrigerator. Isn't it interesting that low-frequency sound resonates in your stomach area and stimulates a hunger response? Is it possible that the refrigerator's drone sound tends to produce a certain hypnotic, trance-like effect? This may account for the zombie-like behavior that many people exhibit when they walk to the refrigerator, open it up, look inside, and then close it, without even being hungry.

Another sound you might not notice at first is the humming of fluorescent lights. Many energy agencies suggest replacing traditional light bulbs with fluorescent lights because they consume less electrical energy. However, the hum of fluorescent lights takes a much larger toll in terms of the physiological energy they drain from us.

Another quiet culprit is the 15,575-cycle-per-second, high-frequency whine of many television sets. This sound is caused by the scan-line circuitry that creates the image on the tube. It is more noticeable on some brands than others. If you develop a headache from watching television, it might be due to this scan-sound. To "cure" your headache, you might try switching to a different TV set.

Some sound-sensitive people are bothered by the hiss of pilot lights on gas ranges and furnaces. One man solved his problem by changing his heating system to a portable, closed-pipe hot water heating system, which was silent and electric.

Making a Difference

Unfortunately, when it comes to noise problems in the community, all too many of us in the post-industrial age tend to take them as facts of life that cannot be changed. There is no need to accept that helpless stance. Each of us can make a difference in controlling noise pollution. People concerned about environmental protection need to recognize that combined efforts have proved successful in the past and they can again produce success in the future.

Consider, for example, the record of the Audubon Society and other conservation groups around the country. They have been victorious in a number of very significant programs, from preventing off-shore drilling to preventing slaughter of wild fowl in the Everglades.

Letters to members of Congress can profoundly affect the nation's air, water, and sound quality. A simple message in your own words directed to senators and representatives will indeed be read and recorded.

Letters and phone calls are useful and necessary, but alone may not be sufficient to ensure success. Good organization, cooperation with other groups, lobbying, legal action, publicity, and fundraising all play a part in making a change.

The idea of people making a change in their lives and in their community is not new. It has worked in controlling water pollution and air pollution. It can also work in controlling sound pollution. In America, this is our heritge and our right.

Chapter 3

SOUND NUTRITION

Digesting Noise

What happens when we not only *ingest* sound but *digest* it, when we not only take it in through our ears but assimilate it into our bodies? What effects can sound have on the physical body besides those it has on the mechanisms of the ear? Some sounds and noises seem to be harmful to the body. Some seem to be therapeutic. How can we learn to distinguish the difference? Let's look at the negative effects first.

At least 9 million people in the United States·live in the direct traffic pattern of high-intensity aircraft engines.

Cracked windows, rattling crockery, and drowned-out conversations may be only the most obvious troubles for people who live with airport noise. Constant exposure to the roar and whine of aircraft, according to the reports of two acoustical researchers at UCLA, may represent a serious hazard to health.

William Meecham and Neil Shaw studied disease and death statistics over a two-year period in the late 1970s among people who lived within a two- or three-mile radius of the Los Angeles International Airport. The residents in this area were exposed to noise levels of 90 to 115 dBA about 560 times each day.

Meecham and Shaw compared results to a similar population living eight to nine miles from the noisy airstrip. The mortality rate from all cases among the near-airport residents was 20 percent higher than for those living farther away; admissions into mental hospitals were 31 percent higher; and cases of cirrhosis of the liver due to drinking were 140 percent higher.

"Everyone knows that loud, intermittent, or continuous noise is disturbing," says Meecham. "Nothing else in our study could account for the increase in mortality."

The California researchers' findings support other similar studies in Los Angeles, Great Britain, and Japan: noise-induced stress can lead to everything from hypertension to nervous breakdowns. Most tragic among these findings is a higher incidence of birth defects. Children suffer from noise more than we realize.

Children and Noise

In 1982, Dr. Sheldon Cohen and his colleagues at the University of Oregon studied children whose schools were along the flight path of Los Angeles International Airport. They found these children had higher blood pressure than similar children attending quiet schools.

The children enduring airport noise abuse also had a more difficult time solving puzzles and math problems and were quicker to give up in frustration. Furthermore, over time, no improvement was noticed in these noise-related effects on the children's abilities. In other words, *the children's bodies never got used to the noise, and the negative effects on their mental abilities remained unchanged.*

Physical Illness and Noise

The ear is not the only organ that can be assaulted and harmed by loud noise. The heart also comes under attack. One of the most notable effects of noise on the human body is the rise in blood pressure. Hypertension, often referred to as a silent killer because it usually has no symptoms, is often a stress-related disease. It can be increased by loud and sustained noise. In fact, cardiovascular functions controlling blood pressure can be adversely affected even by noise levels that don't impair hearing.

In a series of studied funded by the EPA, adult rhesus monkeys were exposed to daily patterns of recorded noises, comparable to those experienced by construction workers using machines such as diesel generators, power drivers, and bulldozers.

In 1981, Dr. E. A. Peterson and his colleagues found that the monkeys' hearing was not affected, but their blood pressure was. Pressure levels in the animals increased 27 percent *and stayed elevated for four months*. The researchers concluded that the effects of noise do not necessarily disappear when the noise stops.

Currently, the EPA is trying to determine whether people working in noisy industries suffer more strokes and heart attacks than workers in quieter environments.

A series of European studies, reported in the *New York Times*, indicated that workers exposed to high noise levels were more likely to develop abnormal heart rhythms, balance disturbances, circulatory ailments, and ulcers. Such workers complained more often of fatigue and irritability.

Noise has been implicated by one research group or another as causing such varied physical conditions as *ulcers; migraine; impotency; infertility; kidney and liver disease; gastrointestinal disturbances; reduced resistance to infectious disease; vertigo; shrinkage of the thymus gland; swelling of the adrenal gland; metabolic stress on the pituitary adrenal complex causing increased adrenocortical activity; vasoconstriction; increased pulse rate; and dilation of pupils.*

Noise and the Central Nervous System

In 1982 researchers James F. Willott and Shao-Ming Lu, from the department of psychology at Northern Illinois University in De-Kalb, found that when laboratory mice were subjected to levels of noise that actually produced hearing loss (at levels not uncommon in our environment), such exposure could not only reduce hearing sensitivity, but could also affect neural coding processes in the brain. After such hearing loss, the animals' central nervous system became more excitable, and an audible stimulus could initiate an abnormal set of events in the brain causing problems of misperception.

In summary, it appears that long-range ingestion of noise creates damage to the ear, disrupts the central nervous system, and creates perceptual distortions in hearing and possibly the other senses.

Unfortunately, there are no tests yet which reveal the body's breaking point, that is, the point at which the noise-induced stress passes the tolerable limit. Noise-sensitivity limits, as we have seen, differ in different people.

Sound Sensitivity

Remarkably, deaf people sometimes are more sensitive to noise than people with normal hearing. Dr. Walter Carlin, Director of the speech and hearing institute at the University of Texas Health Science Center in Houston, said he once went to a disco with two of his deaf friends. They left the place before he did because the intensely high decibel count was creating pain in major organs of their body even though they could not hear.

Noise and Older People

Age may be another variable that can influence how strongly people are affected by noise.

We know that temporary threshold shifts in hearing last longer for older people than for those who are young. A temporary threshold shift occurs when a person's hearing, after being subjected to loud noises, grows dull; after a time, hearing returns to its normal sharpness. In young people the threshold shift process lasts only for a few minutes or hours, at most. But for people over forty, it may take as long as two days for hearing to return to normal.

In general, older people seem to be more susceptible to noise-induced stress. And auditory structures seem to deteriorate on their own as people grow older. This is especially evident in people beyond the age of seventy or seventy-five years. As a rule, the hearing of the elderly is not as acute as that of youngsters. The elderly often have difficulty in understanding speech and have special problems discriminating conversation in noisy surroundings.

A Positive Perspective

Just as certain foods are not harmful to the human body, but nourish and heal it, so certain sounds and music produce no ill effects, but are quite therapeutic. The truth of the saying "Music hath charm to soothe the savage breast" has been known to humanity for thousands of years.

Music Nourishes Animals and Plants

Much research has been done on the positive effects of sound and music on animals and plants.

Egg-laying production among hens has been shown to increase by playing music in the chicken coop. Many farmers claim that piped-in music can help cows produce more milk. The work of Dr. S. K. Bose in India, reported in *The Secret Life of Plants* (1972), showed that the effects of different kinds of music can be distinguished in animal productivity and plant yield per acre.

Plants respond measurably to music. We can "hear" their responses when they are connected to a galvanic skin response (GSR) monitor, and see their growth patterns, over a period of time, in a laboratory.

Researcher Dorothy Retallack set up controlled experiments to test plant response to music. She discovered that certain sounds would actually encourage growth, acting as "sound fertilizer." Although Retallack was mainly interested in measuring leaf growth, root growth, and water absorption, she noticed another phenomenon. When experimental plants seemed to dislike the music, they grew in a direction away from the loudspeakers. When they liked the music, they grew toward the speakers. When classical music of India played in the experimental chambers, the plants literally wrapped themselves around the speakers.

Her plants disliked rock music so much (in particular, the "heavy metal" variety) that some of them withered and died. Plants enjoyed Western classical music, such as Bach, and evidently were delighted with the classical music of India as played by Ravi Shankar.

In 1973, another research group, the Psychotronics Research Institute, looking for ways to soothe, relax, and nourish plants, hooked them up to a GSR device and measured plant response to different kinds of music. They, too, found that by playing certain classical music selections, plants relaxed even more than in their normal environment. When, however, the researchers played *Spectrum Suite*, they reported, "There was a vastly more significant base-line resistance shift than in any other music we were able to test." This meant that the plants were more relaxed with this music than in any other laboratory condition that was tested.

Music and Humans

A recent ad asked, "If Mozart can increase productivity in the chicken farm, what might it do for the office?"

While the ad makes us aware that music can have effects on human well-being and productivity, it may not be true that Mozart is what the ordinary office needs.

To keep people happy and busy, it is not enough to say "music by Mozart." Mozart wrote a lot of music, not all of which fosters happiness and productivity. The same is true of any of the great composers.

In contrast to the highly stylized classical music forms, *Spectrum Suite* is an example of a uniquely new kind of music that contains no recognizable melody, rhythm or harmony, and yet is still musical and aesthetically pleasing. (For further discussion, see Chapter 4, Sound Vibrations.)

We must say which piece and which recording seems to produce the desired effect, and which does not. The reason is that different compositions—or even different versions of the same composition—produce different effects on different people.

The physical effects of a certain selection has little to do with the person's musical tastes or training. The point is that when we ingest sounds, they have an effect on us. The following chapters focus on understanding the ways that sound and music can enhance our lives at the molecular, cellular and organismic levels, as well as the psychological and spiritual levels.

Chapter 4

SOUND VIBRATIONS

Invisible, Inaudible Smog

"You could always tell when Mr. Franiak across the street was shaving," wrote Robert Ebisch, science columnist for *TWA Ambassador* magazine (August, 1983). "It was a morning ritual in the neighborhood. Mr. Franiak turned on his electric razor and the door of his garage went ape, grinding up and back along the ceiling, reversing with a spastic lurch and grinding down again, over and over as long as the razor hummed."

In this chapter, we are not focusing on the high-decibel noise caused by Mr. Franiak's razor or his rumbling garage door, but on the fact that all electrical devices act like antennae and function by using moving and vibrating electrons to perform a job.

An electron is a charged particle with an electrical field that extends in every direction, theoretically to an infinite distance. Vibrating electrons inside the circuits of a shaver, radio, stereo, or a home computer make electromagnetic waves in that field; and unless the component is shielded, those waves move off in all directions like ripples in water. When those waves hit another electrical circuit that responds to the same frequency, they can activate that circuit. Mr. Franiak's razor just happened to make waves that had the same radio frequency as his automatic door opener.

The technical name for this phenomenon is electromagnetic interference (EMI). You have experienced it in radio fadeout when you drive your car under power lines, or when your television picture has been distorted by an airplane passing overhead or a blender being used in the kitchen.

All of the millions of electric circuits sending their vibrations out in all directions is filling the air with an invisible, inaudible electrical smog.

What does this have to do with sound health?

Vibratory Transformers

As human beings, we are sensitive to sounds in ways not even considered by traditional methods. Our bodies are actually living bio-oscillators, much like crystal receiving sets that pick up radio sounds from the environment, or like the circuitry in Mr. Franiak's garage-door opener.

All of us share this planet with vibrating electrical currents. Despite our superficial differences, each of us has a basically similar harmonic hook-up to the universe, based on genetically preprogrammed vibrational patterns coded into our molecular structure. Modern biochemists, astrophysicists, and yogis all agree that at the molecular level of reality, our bodies are systems of vibrating atomic particles.

The cells in our bodies resonate automatically to incoming sound vibrations. During a keynote speech at a Conference on the Nature of Reality in 1976, Dr. William Tiller, Chairman of the Department of Materials Science at Stanford University said, "Each atom and molecule, cell and gland in our body has a characteristic frequency at which it will both absorb and emit radiation."

Thus different parts of our bodies resonate at different frequencies. Each human organ may have its own keynote frequency.

The World of Vibrations

Sound is that which is produced by something vibrating, either randomly or in a periodic, repeated motion.

The human ear connects us with the world of audible sound vibrations. Other senses, such as sight and smell, put us in touch with a vastly wider range of vibrations.

Vibrations in the visible spectrum vibrate between 390 trillion and 780 trillion cycles per second, while the spectrum of human hearing vibrates between approximately 20 and 20,000 cycles per second. By comparison, cells in the ear and throughout the human body rarely vibrate at frequencies that exceed 1000 cycles per second.

But whatever the vibratory spectrum, we can view ourselves— our cells and our senses—as vibratory transformers.

In a very real sense, then, at the core of our physical existence, we are composed of "sound." If we had the proper hearing apparatus, we might even be able to hear our own "harmony." Sensing this biological symphony at the cellular level is beyond the range of most of us, but we do possess a means to experience the vibrational nature of reality.

Sand Shaped by Sound

One of the great pioneers of the field, Swiss scientist Dr. Hans Jenny, devoted ten years to the study of the interrelationship of wave-forms with matter by rendering vibrations into physical forms.

His work, in turn, was based on the discoveries of the eighteenth-century German physicist Ernst Chladni. Chladni scattered sand on steel discs and observed the changing sand patterns produced by playing different notes on a violin.

Greatly expanding on Chladni's work, Jenny scattered liquids, powders, and metal filings on discs, and obtained precise frequency stimuli by using calibrations of a vibrating crystal. Wondrously, as the pitch ascended the musical scale, the harmonic patterns on the discs also changed. Many of the patterns evoked took organic shapes such as the pentagonal stars of sea urchins, the hexagonal cells of honeycombs, the vanishing spirals of the nautilus, and many more. Jenny gave the name "cymatics" to the study of patterns of shape evoked by sound.

Perhaps the forms of snowflakes and the faces of flowers take their shape because they are resonating to some sounds in nature. Perhaps crystals, plants, and even human beings are in some sense music that has taken on visible form.

Perhaps, in some sense, these vibrations maintain life itself.

It is quite possible, as Laurence Blair suggests in his *Rhythm of Vision* (1975), that the geometrical and vortical forms appearing on Dr. Jenny's discs do so because they symbolically represent an underlying order of the physical universe and human consciousness.

Jenny observed that as long as a pitch remains constant, the figure in sand maintains itself. But when the pitch is changed, the pattern inverts itself into a moving one.

Standing Waves

At any moment there are actually two patterns on the disc: the one formed by the sand, and the one formed by the background, which is free of sand. What we normally view as the true pattern (the sand) may not really be so, because the sand collects in areas which are *not* vibrating. The life of the pattern is vibrating in what we call the background (between the sand particles). As Blair put it, "The paradox is that the visible expression of energy is the inverse of the actual vibrationary pattern, which is invisible." It is as if the sand represents a pause, or resting place, in the otherwise vibrating disk.

Technically, the sand reveals a standing wave. The idea of a standing wave is easily grasped if we recall the familiar high school science experiment that involves stretching a string on a wood frame. If the middle of the string was plucked, it formed two symmetrical arcs. If the string was plucked at one-quarter of its length, it formed four symmetrical arcs. These arcs are called standing waves.

In the first case, the string has a point in the middle at which the string is at rest, as well as at the two other points where it is attached to the frame. These three points at rest are called nodes. In the second case, with four symmetrical arcs, there will be five nodes, three on the string and two more where the string is attached to the frame. When the nodes appear stationary while the rest of the string is vibrating up and down, this is called a standing wave.

Musical Spiders

Standing waves are a common phenomenon in nature. Even spiders know how to use them. According to James Bogh in his book *Arachne Rising*, spiders, in building webs, can and must produce visual patterns from sound. If they did not do this, they would get stuck in their own webs.

Here's how they do it. Along the strands of a finished web are evenly spaced droplets of a sticky substance. The even spacing of the droplets, however, is not done by measurement or sight. Rather, the spider simply coats the entire strand of the web with sticky liquid, and then plucks it.

When plucked, the strand of the web produces a standing wave. Standing waves automatically divide the length and width of a string (or metal disc) into an integral number of half wavelengths. Thus, the resulting vibration arranges the droplets at perfectly equal intervals.

Standing waves cannot exist except in an integral number of half wavelengths. Any fractional wavelength cannot be sustained. World-renowned pioneer in bio-medical engineering Itzhak Bentov says in his book *Stalking the Wild Pendulum* (1977), "When a structure is in resonance (which means that it vibrates at a frequency that is natural to it and most easily sustained by it), it implies the presence of a standing wave."

The human body vibrates, too. Each beat of the heart shakes the entire body, and the body responds to this beat. Its response may be measured by a miniature seismograph.

The ejection of blood from the heart's left ventricle causes a peak on the graph, while the portion between the peaks appears rather jagged and irregular. This occurs because the entire body vibrates due to the action of the blood in the aorta, the largest artery in the body.

However, when we hold our breath, the irregular graph assumes a smooth and regular pattern, almost like a sine wave. The reason for this surprising change is that the heart-aorta system has become a resonant system, in which the length of the aorta forms one-half of a wavelength of this system.

Recall that when a structure is in resonance, it implies the presence of a standing wave. While we are breathing regularly, the pressure fronts of returning pulses collide with newly pumped blood somewhere in the aorta, thus producing interference patterns and, consequently, irregular lines on the graph.

However, while the breath is held, the echo and pulse move out of the heart together, and they continue to move up and down synchronously. During these periods the system is said to be in resonance. On the graph, it produces regular, large-amplitude sine waves, about three times stronger than when breathing normally. To sustain this resonant behavior requires a minimum amount of energy.

Itzhak Bentov is one of the shining lights in this field of resonant systems. His research and writing have had a particularly powerful and personal effect on my life. In his book *Stalking the Wild Pendulum*, he asserts, "If we were to ask the brain how it would like to be treated, whether shaken at a random, irregular rate, or in a rhythmic, harmonious fashion, we can be sure that the brain, or for that matter the whole body, would prefer the latter."

Fortunately, we can establish this resonant body state without holding our breath. A number of other techniques, such as meditation, biofeedback, and listening to truly meditational and relaxing music, seem to work just as well.

Sympathetic Vibration

Resonance may be approached in another way. Suppose we have two tuning forks designed to vibrate at the same pitch, say 440 cycles per second. If we strike one of them to produce a sound, the second one will spontaneously start to vibrate. It acts as if it, too, were physically struck. In a way, of course, it was—by the sound waves emanating from the first tuning fork. When this happens we say that the second resonates responsively to the tune of the first. It can do this because it contains within it the required similarity of vibrational makeup that allows for a concordance to make itself heard. We also say the two forks are in sympathetic vibration.

In dealing with sympathetic resonance between two tuning forks tuned to 440 cycles per second, the energy transfer from one to the other occurs because the energy comes to the second fork at its own natural frequency. Such a system, made up of two similarly tuned forks, is called a resonant system.

On a molecular level, atoms are known to be resonant systems. Here the nuclei are like the first tuning fork, and the electrons in their orbits are like the second; they are seen as the reverberations and echoes of the harmonic motions of the nucleus.

Individual atoms and molecules have vibration as their fundamental characteristic.

We know that crystals, violins, bodily organs—in fact, all physical matter—produce detectable "tones."

The phenomenon of resonance, or sympathetic vibration, is not contingent on volume, but on pitch. As long as an object contains within itself the proper vibrational capacity, it can be "played" by outside stimuli in harmony with its vibrational makeup. Thus even quiet sounds, such as the hum of fluorescent lights or televisions, may be able to "play" in resonance upon the cells and molecules of our bodies, as if they were particles of sand on a Chladni disc.

If sand particles can arrange themselves in the presence of pure musical vibrations, is it not possible that musical vibrations, made by musical instruments or our own voices, can have an effect on how the cells of our body are arranged?

The April 24, 1984 issue of *Science News* includes a very important confirmation of these points. Scientists have now discovered that DNA molecules oscillate in resonance in microwaves. Thus the existence of non-thermal, genetic effects from low-level microwaves is quite possible.

The new data are sure to add to the already controversial debate about the bio-effects of "electronic-smog" that is produced by a growing number of electro-magnetic devices, including microwave ovens, broadcast towers, radar installations and high-voltage pow-

er lines. These non-thermal means of absorption—through resonance—are highly controversial, since they are thought to occur at
relatively low power levels, to which a larger segment of the population might be exposed.

In the same article in *Science News*, Mays Swicord, a biophysi-
cist with the National Center for Devices and Radio-Logical
Health at the Food and Drug Administration (FDA), suggested
that this is doubly worrisome because "the DNA molecule is about
the worst place in the body you'd want resonant absorption."

Natural Resonators

We hear and ingest sounds with more than our auditory mechanism. The whole body responds to sound and consumes it whether
we consciously hear the sound or not. Consider how the mind tunes
out the ticking of a clock or the humming of a refrigerator. But
even though the conscious mind can filter out the sound, the body
cannot.

The body responds to sound. This is a law of the physical world,
and it seems to hold true whether the sounds are positive and life-
enhancing or negative and debilitating.

Unfortunately, many of the sounds that assault, audibly or in-
audibly, are not designed to be in harmony with our human vibrational system. X-rays are a common example of inaudible harmful
vibrations, the buzzing of fluorescent lights a common example of
unhealthy audible sounds.

It has been shown that the entire body as a total system vibrates
at a fundamental rate of approximately 7.8 to 8 cycles per second
(inaudible) when it is allowed to come into its most natural, relaxed
state of being. The frequency of brain waves produced in this deeply relaxed (alpha) state, as in meditation, is also in the 8 cycles per
second range.

This is no accident. Physicists have shown that the earth itself
vibrates at this same fundamental frequency of 8 cycles per second.
This is known as the Schumann resonance, and is a function of the
speed of electro-magnetic radiation divided by the circumference

of the earth. The nervous systems of all life forms are attuned to this fundamental frequency. Thus there is a resonance between the human instrument in a natural relaxed state and the electrically charged layers of the earth's atmosphere.

This suggests that the phrase "*being in harmony with oneself and the universe*" might be more than a beautiful, poetic image.

It seems, then, that the more successful we are in creating environments in which the sound stimuli—whether electronic, mechanical, or musical—are in harmony with the vibrational patterns coded into our bodies, the greater our portion of energy, happiness, and sound health will be.

It is indeed marvelous to realize how our bodies both create and resonate to vibrations.

Dr. Peter Manners is an osteopathic physician in Bredford, England. Like Dr. Jenny, he calls himself a cymatologist, and cites an illustration of acoustic-range sound frequencies generated by a human body.

In his article "The Future of Cymatic Therapy" in *Technology Tomorrow* (June, 1980), Dr. Manners claims that contractions of a striated skeletal muscle involve actual vibrations of sound, which, with the aid of a delicate microphone, can be made audible to an observer as a muscle "tone." Similarly, research demonstrates that the liver vibrates at a different frequency from the heart.

According to Dr. Manners, this means that "all processes taking place in the active muscles are organized as vibrations; chemical, energetic, di-electrical, and structural processes follow patterns of regularity imposed by vibrations."

Imposed Vibrations

Dr. Manners goes on to say that "careful observation of structures excited by vibration and sound show that, when they move, they invariably move as a whole. They do not disintegrate or fragment, but move collectively. It is legitimate to speak of a total or wholistic process."

Cymatics and the use of sound in medicine will undoubtedly become a very important study for the future. The human body, as well as each particular organ in it, is not a random heap of matter, but a well-organized entity. Like all objects, the body radiates sound waves and creates sonic fields. Each individual has her or his own different pattern or collection of tones and frequencies. Each of us plays our own unique melody and creates our own unique harmony, as part of the universal harmony.

If Dr. Manners's hypothesis is true, it seems likely that, for example, the liver will grow in the human body in harmony with its vibratory pattern, and with the pattern of its surrounding organism, and with the surrounding wave-pattern of the environment.

"Suppose," suggests Dr. Manners, "that into this field enters an alien impulse, which vibrates in dissonance with the pattern of the liver." Two things can presumably happen.

The first is a sort of imposed vibration. The alien vibration will produce discord and will influence, by its own vibration, the molecular motions of the liver—shifting their phase, enhancing some vibratory component while nullifying others. This deviation from the liver's original harmony would produce stress and, if sustained for a sufficiently long time, possibly ill health.

In the second possible outcome, the liver's vibrations are strong enough, that is, its amplitude is at full strength and unhampered by previous alien impulses. Then it will resist, and will finally force the new impulse to vibrate at the liver's rate and pattern. In this case, the stronger vibration will only slightly dampen the vibration of the liver's molecules.

There is actually a third possibility. If the alien vibration should find a resonating component for itself in the liver's vibratory pattern, as Mr. Franiak's razor found in the garage-door opener's circuitry, then it will acquire strength and will eventually be able to impose its own vibration on the liver. In time, this may even create a new molecular arrangement, probably detrimental to the harmony of the organ and to the harmony of the whole body. Thus its health will be disturbed.

Exercise: A Sound Experience

To see how different areas of your body vibrate to different pitches, sing a low note with your own voice. Use the vowel sound "ah." Let yourself be relaxed and sing the note comfortably and loudly. As you hold the note, close your eyes and with your hand feel where in your body you seem to experience this tone. Move your hand around. If you are relaxed, some parts of your body may begin to vibrate.

Next, using the same vowel sound, sing and hold a medium-range note. See where you feel this tone resonating in your body.

Finally, sing a high note using that vowel sound, and see where its vibrations can be felt.

Most of the people with whom we've worked feel the low notes resonating in the lower parts of their bodies, the middle register tones resonating in the chest cavity and throat, and the high tones localizing themselves in the sinus cavities and head areas.

Therapeutic Applications

During the past decade, the use of ultrasound (sound waves) to visualize and assess the health of unborn children has grown from a rarity to a commonplace. Ultrasound, like X-rays, help us to see where the eyes cannot see, and thus is an excellent diagnostic tool.

However, ultrasound waves are also vibrational frequencies bombarding a human being. Extended exposure to X-ray has been found to damage molecular structure of cells. How safe is ultrasound exposure before birth? Are cells physically altered by ultrasound?

Dr. Robert Mendelsohn, M.D., author of *Confessions of a Medical Heretic* (1979), associate professor of preventive medicine in the School of Medicine at the University of Illinois, and chairman of the Medical Licensing Committee for the State of Illinois, claims that in the fetus, ultrasound causes destruction of DNA cells and delayed maturation.

On the other side of the coin, Dr. Doreen Liebeskind and her colleagues at the Albert Einstein College of Medicine in New York City explored the same question. She exposed fibroblasts (connective tissue cells) from mice to ultrasound of the same intensity as that used on human fetuses. In fact, the same ultrasound machines were used in their experiments as are used on human fetuses. They found that the ultrasound transformed only a few of the total number of cells. Transformation is sometimes an early step toward a cell becoming cancerous, but with the small number of transformed cells, Dr. Liebeskind felt, diagnostic ultrasound does not pose any immediate cancer danger to human fetuses.

Since more research is needed on this issue, it seems that at this point expectant mothers have a right to informed consent when physicians recommend ultrasound for diagnostic reasons.

For our purposes, it is enough to note the apparent confirmation of Dr. Manners's hypothesis that an imposed vibration can indeed create disharmony and even transformation at the molecular and cellular level.

Music Therapy in the 1980s

Is it not also possible to project onto the body a supportive resonance or vibratory pattern to which the body could attune itself? If the body were already in harmony, wouldn't such supportive vibration enhance that harmony? And if the body were out of harmony, couldn't a corrective wave-form help the body retune itself and overcome any invasion within it?

Recent reports from the All-Union Research Institute in the Soviet Union say: "Some oscillation, when applied to the human body, will effect a micro-massage of tissues and cells which will effect a balance and improve blood circulation, metabolism, and the pulsing of the nervous system and endocrine glands."

And from a London hospital report: "It has been found that certain wounds heal in two-thirds of normal time when bombarded with sound waves."

It is evident that sound is destined to play a large part in the future of human health. It may even provide a new paradigm for fostering health.

A Music That Transcends

Music as an energy can have an effect on an individual's body. It can speak to it in vibrational language, helping bring that body into physical alignment and attunement with its own pattern or resonance.

There can be a music that transcends personal tastes, a music to which the nervous system wants to dance, a music that does not require intellectual analysis or emotional involvement.

Certain contemporary nontraditional compositions like *Spectrum Suite* seem to do precisely this.* In this style of music, there is no recognizable melody to hum, and no harmonic progressions to which we have been conditioned to respond. Unlike virtually all other music, there is no central rhythm that hooks us, consciously or unconsciously, to its pulse.

Using tools that already exist in our Western musical system, there is great potential for balancing and relaxing the body and mind.

---

*A fuller discussion of related research may be found in my book *Tuning the Human Instrument* (1978), as well as in my master's thesis *Towards a Contemporary Psychology of Music*, Lone Mountain College, San Francisco, 1973.

Chapter 5

SOUND RELAXATION

Entrainment

Over three hundred years ago, the Dutch scientist Christian Huygens noticed that two pendulum clocks mounted side by side tended to swing together in a matched rhythm. Huygens observed that the two pendulums would maintain this matched rhythm far beyond the mechanical accuracy of the two clocks. To the Dutch scientist, there seemed to be a kind of sympathy between the two clocks, as if they wanted to keep time together.

Huygens was observing what scientists today label "entrainment." Entrainment is another of the major principles to be considered when we seek to understand how the human body responds to sounds.

In the previous chapter we explored the phenomenon of resonance and the science of cymatics. Resonance and entrainment are related. Resonance is a natural vibratory reality occurring on atomic, cellular, and molecular levels. Entrainment is an event that happens between two or more vibrating realities when they come into step, or in phase, with each other. Such an in-phase system can resonate.

Technically, entrainment is the mutual phase-locking of two oscillators. An *oscillator* is any object that pulses or vibrates in a regular, periodic manner. Anything that vibrates produces a "sound" (whether it is audible or not) and alters its environment by creating periodic waves. The "environment" being altered may be body tissue, the heart, a lake, the air, an electrical field, or anything else.

Entrainment is a universal phenomenon. Thus, whenever two or more oscillators in the same field are vibrating at *nearly* the same time, they tend to shift their pulse so that they are vibrating at *exactly* the same time.

Living organisms are oscillators. Like Christian Huygen's pendulums, when they are vibrating at nearly the same frequencies, they tend to lock in together. Entrainment is happening in our bodies at all levels.

"The simplest single-celled organism oscillates to a number of different frequencies, at the atomic, molecular, sub-cellular, and cellular levels," writes George Leonard in *The Silent Pulse*. "Microscopic movies of these organisms are striking for the ceaseless, rhythmic pulsation that is revealed. In an organism as complex as a human being, the frequencies of oscillation and the interactions between those frequencies are multitudinous."

George Leonard recalled an electrifying moment in the film *The Incredible Machine* when he watched two individual muscle cells from the heart through a microscope. At first, he said, each cell was pulsing with its own rhythm. Next, the two cells moved closer together. Just before they touched, there was a momentary shift in the rhythm and then they were pulsing together in perfect synchronicity. Entrainment had been captured on film.

But what has this to do with relaxation and music?

Relaxation at the Cellular Level

"Relaxation" may be described as being in harmony with oneself and with the world.

If we look at our bodies as bioresonators, we are relaxed when our physical system is operating in resonance; when our actions are being carried out seemingly effortlessly with a minimum expenditure of energy; or when a high degree of biorhythmic entrainment is going on among the oscillators within the organism.

But because our organism is made up of complex sets of oscillators, we are also subject to entrainment with the outside world. When the body experiences vibrations from the outside that are nearly at the same pulse as some part of the organism, entrainment is likely. If the frequency of the outside stimulus is powerful and consistent enough, the organism is likely to be entrained to the same pulse as the outside source, and lose its own natural rhythm. In a sense, then, the organism goes out of tune with itself.

For example, as we listen to music we enjoy, we may claim that it relaxes us. It is likely in this case that the musical selection and its enjoyment is a function of familiarity. We tend to like what is familiar. We may express our enjoyment by making associations to the music, recalling memories it brings up, or following its melody line.

In a series of landmark studies conducted in 1973, and summarized in *Field Effects of Music on the Electromagnetic Energy Body*, researchers at the Psychotronic Research Institute in California (including Dan Kientz, Randall Fontes, and myself) discovered some interesting facts about relaxation and music. We discovered that the music that people thought was relaxing them was, in fact, not relaxing them to any physiologically significant degree.

In the experiments carried out, even though a high percentage of subjects subjectively labeled the mood of Lizst's *Liebestraum No. 3* as "highly relaxing, soothing and meditative"* their objective relaxational response was very much less than expected. Physiological response parameters tested included electrical conductivity of the skin measured by GSR and electromagnetic energy fields measured by Kirlian photography.† In neither test were the subject's responses shifted by the Lizst selection into levels associated with deep relaxation. In fact, the scientific equipment detected a high level of non-relaxed brain activity.

So, although their subjective verbal responses described the mu-

---

*Certain classical selections were defined as "relaxing/meditative/soothing" by the Music Research Foundation, an agency set up by the Surgeon General's Office. The foundation had its origins shortly after World War II, when the federal government was searching for non-drug modalities in the treatment of shell-shocked veterans.

†Kirlian photography, developed by the Russian scientist Semyon Davidovich Kirlian, is a technique that uses high-voltage and high-frequency electromagnetic energy, beyond the ultraviolet range, to produce an image of the energy field surrounding an animate or inanimate object on photographic film in total darkness without a lens.

sic as soothing and relaxing, their bodies' objective responses—
their relaxational coordinates—were very much less than expected.

Music for Relaxation

Most music is not consciously composed to be relaxing or healing. It is not surprising, therefore, that the effects of such music are
not truly relaxing or healing.

This is not to say that such music is not good. It does, however,
suggest that we might do well to use the appropriate music for the
desired response. Indeed, it appears that much more is involved in
choosing music that is truly relaxing than simply finding selections
that most people think are relaxing, meditative, or soothing. By the
same token, the potentials for creating a program of sound health
are much greater than we have been led to believe.

In addition to testing classical music defined as relaxing and
soothing, Kientz, et al. also tested *Spectrum Suite*. In test subjects,
this music produced a dramatic change in the GSR measurements
and the Kirlian image in ways that indicated significant degrees of
relaxation. Subsequent testing involving electro-acupuncture and
applied kinesiology and kinesionics have corroborated these
results.*

Furthermore, the extraordinary relaxational results of this music proved successful no matter what the age, sex, and education of
the listeners. Thus it facilitated relaxation in young and old, male
and female, those with much education and those with little, regardless of musical tastes.

The beauty of this music is that it fosters health automatically
and effortlessly. The entire body responds naturally to it. At a cel-

---

*Electro-acupuncture is based on the fact that our bodies have a fourth system of
circulation (beside blood, air, and lymph) based on electromagnetism. By measuring the electrical voltage potential at critical points (meridians) along the system,
we can determine whether the system is in a balanced, healthy state. Applied kinesiology, formulated by Dr. George Goodheart and related to acupuncture meridians,
studies the body's response to a variety of stimuli—sound, food, emotions, etc.—by
simultaneously testing the strength of a specific muscle. Kinesionics, developed by
Karta Purkh Khalsa in Seattle, is a synthesis of kinesiology and radionics.

lular level, the musical stimulus seems to be understood and assimilated.

When the parts of the body are in resonance, the body need not be forced to work, but seems to act effortlessly, as if everything were in tune.

It has been my experience that an *externally* imposed rhythm—such as we find with most all music—is rarely as relaxing as a rhythm that is *internally* chosen by the individual's own nervous system.

My sense is that biorhythmic entrainment accounts for a significant part of its positive effects over such a broad spectrum of people. Breathing slows down, the heartbeat becomes more regular, and the mind activity slows down to alpha rhythms.

In short, the relaxation happens on both the physiological as well as the psychological levels. The body, as far as we can tell, seems to be allowed to express its own inner nature and harmony.

Further enhancement of the relaxational effect is afforded by creative visualization of appropriate areas of the body being resonated by the sound. Using music and imagination as a tool to foster psychological well-being will be treated in Part II.

An Apparent Contradiction

It may be helpful here to acknowledge what seems like an apparent contradiction.

On the one hand, Kientz, *et al.*, produced results that seemed to indicate that classical music—even selections designated as relaxing and soothing—may not be the most effective music for relaxing. On the other hand, research results produced by traditional music therapists seem to indicate that classical selections can produce significant relaxation.

How are we to reconcile the two sets of results? A number of factors are involved.

One key factor involves the relative *depth* of the evoked relaxation. Clearly, most people are simply not trained to quantitatively differentiate a deep relaxation state from a mild relaxation state. Without a physiological standard for comparison, almost any music other than punk rock, disco, or heavy metal might be termed "relaxing."

Second, remember that the body want more than anything else to be *balanced*, to be healed, to be whole. It will do all it can to balance and heal itself, given any reasonable help or cue. With the body, a little "sound" help goes a long way. Indeed, the "vibrational common denominator" of such helpful cues might be the sound itself—pure energy—as long as the sound is, so to speak, in the right ballpark.

There is a third factor in dealing with the apparent contradiction in experimental results. As we have said before, people have individual *tastes* in music. What delights one person musically may displease another. Long before subjects took part in a research experiment, many of them were familiar with, and may have learned to relax with, certain kinds of music. This "conditioned learning process" would undoubtedly influence the test results.

This factor reminds us of another vehicle of healing—the mind. The California researchers focused on relaxation without engaging the mind; they measured relaxation at the cellular and molecular levels of the body. When other researchers testing the effects of music engage the emotional, intellective, imaginative, and associative faculties of the mind (as with classical music), psychological responses may be triggered which are also very useful in establishing a healing environment.

From a larger perspective, then, perhaps the two approaches are not mutually exclusive. Both can be successful in helping achieve relaxation, even though each is different and each succeeds for different reasons.

Getting Back in Tune

Deep relaxation and meditation techniques evoke a physiological state that is more healthful than merely "taking a rest." Biofeedback and yoga are among these techniques. But one of the easiest methods to help achieve deep relaxation is listening to music specifically composed for relaxation and meditation.

We foresee such meditational or stress-management music becoming a natural alternative or complement to tranquilizers and sedatives in dealing with simple stress. We do not claim that music-listening can cure every stress-related illness, but it can surely help a good number of them.

Sometimes stress, like the tip of an iceberg, merely indicates a deeper problem, such as a physical illness or a complex psychological disorder. When this is the case, individuals should seek appropriate help from a physician or therapist.

Today, even for people under severe physical or psychological stress, physicians, surgeons, and therapists are beginning to prescribe meditational, musical and guided-imagery techniques to induce relaxation and reduce the need for tranquilizers. Medical researchers report improvement resulting from such relaxation in the quality of life, less drug side effects, fewer accidental deaths, and less money spent on drugs.

Living Harmoniously in a Stressful World

In twentieth-century society, as we have seen, noise levels are frequently such that they can get us out of tune. One reason people are seldom aware that they have been knocked out of tune is that they've never been in tune.

The ever-increasing assault of sound upon us adds to the other stresses that we face at home and on the job. This stress load can be lessened by bringing more relaxation into our lives. *Unfortunately, our environment does not adapt itself to us. We must learn to adapt to it, or change it.*

A first step is to identify which of the elements of our environment can be adjusted to lessen stress and which can be used to counteract the effects of stress, induce relaxation, and ultimately promote health.

By understanding how sound and music can affect our bodies,

emotions, and minds, we can begin to institute effective changes in our lives. These changes can counteract the negative effects of the environment, and prevent our continual manipulation by a whole host of unwelcome external stimuli.

It is time to tune in to yourself, and to assume basic responsibility for getting yourself in tune and keeping yourself in tune.

Begin observing the subtle changes caused in you by sounds. As a preventive measure, this will give you a greater sense of when the environment is wearing down your defenses. Begin to recognize how your physical body and your emotions react to various industrial sounds and noise, and different kinds of music. Only when you learn this will you be able to deal with them in a positive, health-promoting way.

Beginning at Home

One of my favorite axioms of harmonious living is "Sound health begins at home." Relaxation, considered by many medical authorities to be a major condition for attaining and maintaining health, can be easily learned and enjoyed at home.

Why not begin with music? If you've had a day of stressful noise at work, you deserve a treat of enjoyable and relaxing music. Put on a tape or record and fill your environment with relaxing, comforting vibrations. Select what feels right for you.

For purposes of relaxation, listen primarily to soothing music in which the music itself relaxes the nervous system, rather than making the nervous system more nervous. In this way, your body handles the energy flow more efficiently.

Some people find that they can help deal with tension headaches without drugs by allowing themselves to focus totally on the music. This is not an analytical or critical process, but an imaginative one. For example, you might imagine that the music is a soothing stream washing over you. Many people imagine that their tight, tense, or strained muscles are being massaged by the sound waves themselves.

Another technique might be to imagine someone else massaging your throbbing temples or tight shoulders. Let yourself feel the soothing hands as the melodic flow enhances and flows with your breath.

Another approach is to listen to the spaces between the sounds, rather than the sounds themselves.

Yet another is to imagine that you are the instrument that makes the sound. Let yourself feel the vibrations that the musical instrument is feeling as it is played.

Another approach is to imagine that the music is breathing you.

The point in all of these techniques is for you to become totally immersed in the sound.

A New Way to Listen

Most of us have found our own ways of listening to music, principally for entertainment or dancing.

Most of us, too, are accustomed to listening to music in the background and treating the sound as if it were a kind of harmless aural wallpaper.

Those who have studied music academically were taught to listen analytically and critically, that is, by analyzing the form and structure of the music and judging the quality of its technical performance.

But none of these are necessarily modes of listening that are significantly relaxing and therapeutic, nor do they invite fully the uplifting and transcendent aspects of music to be experienced. Most people have never learned how to listen to music in a healing way.

In order to listen to music in a relaxing and therapeutic way, pay attention to the response that your own human instrument gives to the sound stimulus. Does your body and mind grow calm and relaxed? Or do you grow tense and uncomfortable?

In addition to paying attention to the music, pay attention to yourself. Take note of what is happening to you as the music plays.

Listening at Home

Your posture may affect how you hear.

Many people find it helpful either to lie down with knees slightly raised and a folded towel under the neck for support, or to sit upright with hands resting on the legs and palms facing upward, as if receiving a gift.

Experiment. You may discover another posture that is better for you. Try pointing your feet toward the speakers. If you are listening with a partner, try listening feet-to-feet or back to back. In this way your body acts as a sound transducer or amplifier to transfer sound into your partner, and through your partner into you.

Notice if the music to which you listen sounds different in each of these listening formats. You may also notice that the same piece of music sounds different with different listening partners.

Listening in Public

You may use some of these same insights while listening to live music. Obviously, in an auditorium, you cannot use some of the postures recommended for home listening. You also are generally discouraged from expressing the music in your body, or swaying in your seat. But you can explore different ways of listening from the inside that will allow you to derive great benefit from the live concert.

First, consider what you hear.

Each concert or performance, combined with your response to it, is a unique event. What you hear has never been played quite like that before and will probably never be played like that again. There is a subtle interplay of emotional and physical rapport between the performer, you, and the rest of the audience. Why not make the most of it? Live it to the fullest.

You may listen to music with your creative imagination. Close your eyes as you listen. Closing the eyes cuts off external visual stimuli, and thus intensifies the listener's ability to focus on the sound. You are not obliged to keep your eyes on the conductor or on the performers. You can watch your own inner responses to the music. If your imagination is active, you may watch the screen in the movie of your mind.

One of the special qualities of concerts is that you listen not only with your own energy, but with the collective energies of all those in attendance. The amassed attention of an audience creates a large energy field that can affect the sounds being made as well as the way those sounds affect our bodies and minds.

A Paradox

One of the most puzzling paradoxes with respect to deriving benefit from listening to music is witnessed near the end—or sometimes even before the end—of a classical concert. It is harsh, staccato, and earsplitting applause. Isn't it strange that the beauty of the music is shattered by the firecracker-like sounds of the audience?

Similarly, the preponderance of coughing that goes on, particularly in the quiet portions of a concert, gives one cause to consider that perhaps that phenomenon has more going on with it than merely a tickle in the throat. Whether it's because the members of the audience "want to get into the act," and subconsciously want to be "on stage" themselves, or because they can't stand feeling so good and want to sabotage their own good feelings, is not ours to say, but these concerns deserve our consideration.

It would appear that the time is at hand to develop a new way of showing appreciation rather than to destroy the beauty that had just been created. It would be to the benefit of both the audience and the performer to work in such a context.

Give Your Body a Chance

In the final analysis, perhaps it is not important to know whether the music itself is doing the relaxing or if it simply assists the body to relax itself. We do know that the body itself is usually a self-rectifying organism, if we give it a chance. It may be that music is basically amplifying the body's own healing and relaxing abilities. But even at that, music can be a powerful adjunct to the healing process. The bottom line is our own health and well-being!

Therapeutic music may be a lot like aspirin. We don't know fully how aspirin works, only that it appears to work. We use aspirin, why not music?

Today, people have the equipment to sound-condition their

dwellings and workplaces with relaxing and harmonious music. Such music would be more attractive than urban environmental noise to the body's nervous system. Because the body naturally prefers a more harmonious sound, it will likely be the music to which the body responds and attunes itself.

To create a relaxing environment in your home or apartment, you may choose to listen to music, nature sounds, or broadband-masking frequencies.* If you live in an urban environment, recordings of nature sounds may be obtained at most record stores. As for masking devices, there are several on the market (see Sound Helps, at the end of this book).

Music-listening for relaxation is not the only ingredient in a sound diet. In Chapter 7 we suggest ways that you can create and produce sound by yourself—for example, by singing, toning, or making some of your own music on a piano, guitar, or other instrument.

_____

*Broadband-masking frequencies refer to any sound that contains all the frequencies of the audial spectrum, often referred to as "white sound" or "white noise." Examples include a waterfall, wind, rain, ocean surf, or electronic or mechanical imitations of these natural phenomena.

Chapter 6

SOUND MEDICINE

Medicine and Health

John Torinus, editor of the Appleton, Wisconsin *Post-Crescent*, recently spent five days in Appleton Memorial Hospital's cardiac wing "having my heart put back on its proper course." In addition to medicinal treatment, heart surgeon Dr. David Warner prescribed "beautiful music" for Mr. Torinus, and brought him a cassette player and four cassettes to listen to as he relaxed during his hospital stay.

"I found the tapes fascinating," Torinus wrote in his column "Editor's Notebook," Feb. 14, 1982. "And as I listened lying there in a hospital bed, there was no question that they helped immensely to relax me."

Dr. Warner uses such cassettes with his patients before, during, and after surgery. He asks his patients to listen with headphones for several hours before they enter the surgical ward. They keep the headphones on even while anesthetized, the music playing to the unconscious as well as to the conscious mind.

Dr. Warner says he is only in the beginnings of his study of the use of music to help heal the human body.

Health is not just an absence of disease; it is a positive quality of living. It deals with our ability to create, to enjoy, to develop, to function fully, to manifest our full potential in life, love, work, and play.

Holistic medicine is in part a response to the increasing depersonalization in much of modern medicine. Modern medicine tends to emphasize malfunctioning organs and treats the body as a biochemical machine that sometimes needs to be repaired. On the other hand, holistic medicine tends to view the patient as a complete person and attempts to respond, not just to the illness, but to the person's health and total life, including the environment.

In his book *The Psychology of Consciousness*, professor of psychology at University of California at San Francisco, Robert Ornstein, Ph.D., hits the nail on the head when he says that, "Our medical endeavor is primarily directed towards the treatment of diseases, not toward individual responsibility for health. We attempt to control bodily problems from the outside with drugs rather than attempting to employ the individual's built-in capacity for self-regulation."

While a physician's focus is on curing a disease and helping prevent future problems with it, a health specialist's focus is on helping us thrive in our own unique ways. In talking about health care, we aren't necessarily just talking about doing things *to* people, which is the standard medical perspecitve today. Instead, we put the emphasis on doing things *with* them, that is, having the patient take a conscious role in his own healing and growth.

Music and Healing

Much of what people talk about as healing today is really self-healing. Indeed, many doctors admit that they themselves don't do the healing; they merely help get rid of a problem that is keeping the body from healing itself. Used appropriately, music can often facilitate healing, though the actual way music is used may vary considerably.

Music in Hospitals

Some hospitals are now allowing—and inviting—music inside their walls. For example, at the Kaiser-Permanente Medical Center in Los Angeles, California, patients in pain can turn not only to prescriptions but to periods of soothing music and guided relaxation on a tape player. Some of the center's doctors even "prescribe" music tapes instead of pain killers and tranquilizers.

"We tell patients to use this tape anytime they need it," comments

Dr. David Walker, a staff psychiatrist specializing in behavioral medicine, "just before they are wheeled into the operating room, or even as the doctors are talking to them. They can replay the tape in their minds, even if they can't listen to it, and get the same results."

At Kaiser-Permanente in Oakland and San Francisco, relaxation music and guided relaxation with music are being used before cardiac surgery, during chemotherapy, with chronic back pain patients, and for crippling spinal injuries. Outpatients with stress-related illnesses such as high blood pressure, migraine headaches, and ulcers are encouraged to do the same music-and-relaxation training.

Having music available throughout the hospital, rather than just in music therapy wards, is a relatively new development. As far as we can tell, it was encouraged by patients who were familiar with relaxation music tapes and brought them along into the hospital and operating room. They noticed, without anyone telling them, that the music helped them relax. Hearing this music, doctors and nurses—as well as other patients—grew interested in it. They were especially intrigued with its beneficial effects.

Personally, innoculating the institutional environment with music has been one of the most delightful and satisfying aspects of my work.

The Hospital Atmosphere

Kaiser-Permanente is only one of several facilities that have been successfully using relaxation music to reduce stress, relieve pain, and help personalize the often sterile atmosphere of the hospital. Notable among them are the University of Massachusetts Medical Center in Worcester, Massachusetts; Beth Israel Hospital in Boston, Massachusetts; Hahnemann University Hospital in Philadelphia, Pennsylvania; the Walter Reed Army Medical Center and Mount Zion Hospital in San Francisco, California; A.R.E. Medical Center in Phoenix, Arizona; and the Simonton Cancer Research and Counseling Center in Dallas/Fort Worth, Texas.

Doctors William and Gladys McGarey at the A.R.E. Medical Center in Phoenix report that music is being used in the birth room, the biofeedback room, the counseling room, the massage rooom, and during physical therapy, as well as in the waiting room and gift shop.

In one hospital, music is helping to enable a stroke victim to speak again. In another center, it is helping burn victims deal with pain as their burns heal. In a third, it is helping a cancer patient with chronic pain.

Some music programs tend to evoke imagery, others develop a state of detachment. Most help to reduce the physical concomitants of stress such as high blood pressure and fast heart rate.

Music has been used in childbirth and delivery, and to help teach methods of relaxation to be used during childbirth as well as in the weeks before the baby comes. There are many reports from happy mothers who describe how their labor and birth process was greatly facilitated when accompanied and orchestrated by music.

In hospices, music is being used to help people knit together the unraveled strands of their lives. Music therapy is useful in summarizing life and preparing for death. It also assists people in dealing with their grief over the death of a loved one.

How the Music is Delivered

In the early 1970s, cassette players were relatively new. They were designed for recording the spoken voice and produced poor sound quality, especially with music. Nevertheless, patients took their cassette players with them to the hospital. And no matter how poor the sound fidelity was, the music seemed to work for them.

Now, with the development of personal stereo systems and headsets, patients can immerse themselves in the music. They can enjoy high quality sound without annoying their neighbors.

In some hospitals, special programs of relaxing music are being broadcast through the public address system, making the music available to entire wards.

With this in mind, I have created several programs of long-playing tapes, which contain up to eight hours of continuous, relaxing music. They are specifically designed for long-duration situations such as lengthy operations, labor time before childbirth, or postoperative recovery.

The unique nature of this genre of music is such that one cannot fully remember it or recognize it. It avoids the identifiable structure of most traditional music, so that no matter how often you hear it, it's as if it were for the first time.

Music Rx®

Music therapist Helen L. Bonny, founder of the Institute for Consciousness and Music, has also designed a set of taped listening programs, called *Music Rx*, for use in a wide variety of hospital settings. Through research and testing, she put together programs of music designed to create "reduction of stress, a pleasant diversion, and a quieting of mood state." Her programs utilize the music of classical composers such as Bach, Haydn, Tchaikovsky, Mendelssohn, Vivaldi, Respighi, Walton, Vaughn-Williams, Marcello, Dvorak, Debussy, Massenet, Bizet, and Britten.

Music Rx is an outgrowth of fifteen years of research done by Dr. Bonny. While studying the effects of music on the body and emotions, she has worked with both "normal" and psychiatric patients, as well as with hospitalized cancer patients and narcotic addicts. Interest in music for hospitalized persons was generated by her own experience as a coronary care patient. Her first tests for the *Music Rx* programs were run on herself.

Music Rx was tested in two six-month-long pilot projects at two hospitals, Jefferson General Hospital in Port Townsend, Washington, and St. Agnes Hospital in Baltimore, Maryland. The project, which included both patients' and nurses' responses, were centered in the intensive care units.

Results showed a measurable reduction of heart rate in patients after listening to music programs. Psychological ratings showed positive effects on depression and anxiety as well as relief of pain.

Nurses reported positive patient responses, such as lowering of blood pressure and pulse, regular deep breathing, closed eyes, relaxed muscles, and sleep. For some, the music evoked pleasant memories and nurtured positive moods.

With music playing in the patient's headsets, nurses found it easier to change intravenous needles, move patients from one bed to another, or place patients on a respirator.

Dr. Richard R. Lynn, director of the coronary care unit at Jefferson General Hospital, commented on Bonny's music program, "It added an element of *humaneness* in an otherwise mechanical, sterile environment."

Music and Medicine Today

"Throughout history," writes Dr. David E. Bresler in *Free Yourself From Pain*, "music has been incorporated into many healing rituals. In recent scientific studies, music has been shown to accelerate body metabolism, muscular activity and respiration. It also influences pulse rate and blood pressure, and minimizes the effects of fatigue. Other studies suggest that music may even break down cholesterol in the blood stream."

If sound and music are so effective in promoting healing, why isn't it more widely used?

There are several reasons. One is that students in medical school receive little or no training in the therapeutic effects of sound and music. Unfortunately, many medical students are told that unorthodox forms of healing are mere quackery.

Dr. Robert Mendelsohn, in his book *Confessions of a Medical Heretic*, suggests that the lack of interest in alternative healing modalities comes from the desire of organized medicine to maintain political control and monopoly. For the record, some of the types of healing that have come under fire from the American Medical Association (AMA) in the past decade include chiropractic, acupuncture, the use of vitamin supplements and megavitamin therapy, light and color therapies, and psychic and native healers.

But the AMA does not speak for all its members. Some carry on their own personal "holistic" explorations, without labeling them as such.

We are also witnessing a new phenomenon. Many physicians have joined the American Holistic Medical Association (AHMA), founded and organized in the late 1970s by Dr. Norman Shealy. The AHMA physicians are openly incorporating in their practice a wide range of alternative healing modalities, including music.

Outside the United States

Using sound and music in the healing process has become accepted practice in many countries outside the United States. Sound healing is an integral part of the health delivery system in such countries as Canada, Mexico, Great Britain, and the Soviet Union.

In researching material for their book *Aging and Mental Health*, co-authors Myrna I. Lewis and Robert N. Butler, M.D. were amazed when they visited several Soviet sanitariums near the Black Sea and found aging Soviets, with both physical and mental illnesses, being treated not with drugs but with vibrations. The healing prescription included specially designed music played into patients' rooms and the sound of the sea recorded on tapes.

Four Views of the Human Body

One historical approach to medicine sees the human body as a kind of *mechanical system* of levers and pulleys, so that when arms, legs, muscles, or joints are broken or sprained they must be "lubricated" or "repaired."

A second approach to medicine sees the body as a kind of *plumbing system* of blood circulation, ingestion, digestion, and the like. When things go wrong with the plumbing, it must be "cleaned" or "cut and mended" in the hospital's operating room.

For the last few decades the focus of medicine has been to view the human body as a *chemical system*, so that if something goes awry it may be cured by adding a certain chemical, drug, or other substance to the person's chemical makeup.

Most recently, researchers are discovering that the body is also an *electromagnetic system*—in other words, an oscillating system or system of vibrations. And here is where sound comes in.

The Body Electric

Several years ago, Robert F. Becker of Upstate Medical Center in Syracuse, New York, showed that electrical fields applied to slow-mending bone fractures can enhance healing. Dr. Becker also made news when he showed evidence that partial limb regeneration in mammals was possible if oscillating electrical fields were applied to the stump of the amputated arm or leg.

Biologists knew that more primitive life forms, such as the salamander, will regenerate an amputated leg, whereas a rat cannot. Becker found that the capacity to self-regenerate the lost limb was indeed possible to a rat—at least partially—when appropriate electrical fields were applied to the stump at the right moment in the healing cycle.

Recently, three researchers at the University of Connecticut School of Medicine in Farmington—Gideon A. Fodan, Lizabeth Bourret, and Louis Norton—have reported that oscillating electrical fields caused DNA synthesis in cartilage cells. They were able, under a pulsed direct current external electrical field oscillating at 5 hertz, to invariably stimulate the incorporation of thymidine into the DNA molecule.

The therapeutic importance of this synthesis is its suggestion that the normal communication between cells is not only mediated by the cell membranes, but also involves the flow of ions. Modulating the flow of ions through certain oscillating electrical frequencies can apparently affect the "instruction" to the cells and influence their very makeup.

It also reinforces the usefulness in medicine of viewing the human body as an oscillating system, and opens up new vistas of research in healing and health care through vibratory fields such as light, electricity, magnetism, color, and sound. Some researchers are beginning to explore the possibilities.

Healing Through Resonance and Vibration

As reported in *The Secret Life of Plants*, French engineer Andre Simoneton suggests that if human nerve cells can receive wavelengths, they must also be transmitters. As senders and receivers, they can enter into resonant vibration with each other in order to pick up a transmission.

While Simoneton focused much of his energy testing the radiation of different foods, identifying which had high and healthy radiation and which had low and poor, he also applied his techniques to measuring the wavelengths given off by human beings.

He found that the average healthy person gives off a radiance of about 6,500 angstrom units, while tobacco smokers, alcohol imbibers, and heavy meat eaters give off uniformly lower radiance. Cancer patients give a radiance almost 2,000 units less than normally healthy people. He also found that cancer victims will radiate this low level long before any overt symptoms of disease are present.

Simoneton's dream is that one day physicians, using headsets, will be able to diagnose patients by tuning into the frequencies given off by their ailing organs, and then be able to help cure them by broadcasting more healtful vibrations to the organs.

New Research on Melanin

Dr. Frank Barr, a California physician, in an article "Melanin" in *Medical Hypotheses* (1983) suggests that melanin, a primitive and universal substance known primarily as skin pigment, is the major organizing molecule for living systems. "Melanin and its connections comprise the mind's eyes," is Dr. Barr's way of putting it.

This hitherto long-neglected substance now seems centrally involved in the control of all physiological and psychological activity.

"It's audacious!" exclaims Barr describing the characteristics of melanin. "It's made up of neurotransmitters capable of converting light energy to sound energy and back again."

Not only does melanin (and neuromelanin, the brain's melanin) have the properties of an electrical semiconductor, but it also shows evidence of being a room-temperature superconductor. What's more, it binds and releases other key molecules, and also seems capable of self-synthesis.

Because of melanin's two-way capacity to convert energy—from light to sound and back to light—the melanin model offers a powerful scientific rationale for healing and medical therapies that rely on light, color, sound, biofeedback, acupuncture, visualization, and the like, rather than on drugs and surgery.

Research on melanin as a gateway to healing has only begun.

The Next Great Leap

Direct current energy in various parts of our bodies can be measured through a superconducting quantum interference device (SQUID), a machine that uses liquid helium and can screen out any kind of extraneous electromagnetic interference. "We could perhaps eventually learn to use it, as in biofeedback," Barr points out, "to enhance healing or regeneration once we know what to look for."

"In this case," Barr continues, "your best asset for self-healing would be a subtle ability to shift your consciousness to affect the direct current. You couldn't order someone else to do it for you!"

Dr. John Knowles's observation about personal responsibility, mentioned earlier, echoes the sentiments of Dr. Barr. Knowles said, "The next great leap in the health care of the American people will be when the people learn to take care of themselves."

And if, as Andre Simoneton believes, sounds can be used to help *detect* disease at an early date and help cure it in a noninvasive manner, then it is also possible that humans can learn to follow a healthy diet of sound to *keep* themselves in tip-top shape and in radiant health.

Chapter 7

SOUND DIET

Sickness or Wellness

In 1980 Americans spent almost 10 percent of the gross national product on what is labeled "personal health care." More precisely, this figure—almost 220 billion dollars—is spent on sickness care.

Because of unhealthy lifestyle, many Americans remain stuck in sickness-care when they could and should be into wellness-care.

Guidelines for Owners

Owner's manuals come with car stereos, television sets, and appliances, but not with human bodies. Why is it that we have virtually no training on how the human machine works, or how to make it run more effectively?

We get owner's manuals for all our mechanical and electronic machinery because we believe that the more we know about them to keep them in top condition, the better they perform. One might say that we promote "high-level wellness" in our autos, tools, and appliances. Why not do the same for our most personal vehicle? This chapter presents some guidelines for planning a personal wellness program that makes effective use of sound and music.

When offending sound is in your control, you can act to modify or change it. For example, you can change a phonograph record, change a radio station, turn down the volume of a sound system, or put a sound-absorbing pad beneath your typewriter or refrigerator.

Sometimes stopping unwanted sound or noise is out of your control. In this case, you can still act. You are not helpless. You can close doors between you and the noise, wear ear protection, complain, or simply leave the scene until the noise ceases.

You can also fight back ugly noise with some beautiful music of your own. Put on some taped music to mask the undesirable noise, and set your life to music of your choosing.

Sounds Especially for You

Most of our "sound diet" suggestions apply to the time you take for yourself. This is the time when you use sound and music not merely as background to your life, but as foreground, as the main focus of your consciousness. You are nurturing and nourishing yourself with sound and music—or silence, when that is appropriate.

We suggest that you set aside a specific time for consuming sound "food," much as you would schedule time for dinner or to watch a certain television show. You might prepare for it by taking care of whatever you need to take care of, and letting everything else wait.

For some people, this sound nutrition time becomes so important that they take the phone off the hook, and ask other family members not to disturb them. It is a time to relax and get all parts of the body and mind in harmony again.

Taking a Music Bath

Put the music of your choice on the stereo.

Assume a relaxing posture, take a deep breath, and exhale any tension that may be in your body.

You may choose to lie down with your feet facing the speakers. (I call this a special form of "sole music.") Keep your knees slightly elevated, and your neck supported by a folded towel.

Allow the sound of the music to wash over you, to rinse off all the sound pollution and junk-sound your body was bombarded with today.

Allow yourself to be immersed in the music as you would in a bath. Enjoy the music, noticing how it resonates in different parts of your body.

The more relaxed you become, the more you can enjoy the music. If you need to, take a few more slow, deep breaths, to allow any remaining tension to wash away.

For a deeper and more profound experience, some people prefer to listen to the music with headphones. If you choose this way, you might focus on the sonic image as it shifts from one ear to the other, or from in front of you to behind your head.

Or you might enjoy being aurally massaged—on the inside as well as on the outside—by the different instruments and sound textures as they appear in the orchestration. Let yourself be totally immersed in sound.

Moving without Movement

Another way to be nourished by music is to move *interiorly*—this can happen without physical movement.

Use your imagination to feel the flow of the music's energy and your response to it on a cellular and molecular level. Enjoy letting the cells and molecules of your body dance and move in response to the nourishing vibrations of the musical sound. This can be a very energizing, yet relaxing, experience.

Moving to Music

It is also possible, of course, to respond physically to music. Although the dance exercises and physical workout routines in many health clubs use rock and disco music, we suggest that you try a wide range of tempos and rhythms to evoke a wide range of emotional and physical responses. For exmple, some music and rhythms of the Middle East and Africa invite the body to move in ways that naturally activate, strengthen, and relax the pelvis and thighs.

Changes of movement and posture release energy throughout the body. As the body is energized, it seems more able to digest the sound food that it is receiving.

Music with less focus on rhythm can assist the body in relaxing by opening it up to deep stretching exercises, as in certain yoga postures. The appropriate music seems to reach the body on muscular and molecular levels, allowing it to loosen up and stretch in surprising ways. Such music also helps slow down the breathing and regularize the heartbeat.

Using Sound Nutrition

Kinesiologists have discovered that longer musical passages have an effect upon the muscles. It also seems clear, though much research is still called for, that tonal sequences, short motifs, and even isolated tones can evoke a strong response at the cellular level.

In food nutrition, amino acids are the basic building blocks of the more complex proteins. The body is usually able to digest the different amino acids found in fruits, vegetables, and grains more easily than the complex proteins found, for example, in meats. Sound nutrition seems to work in a similar way.

In the context of "sound nutrition," individual tones, motifs, and tonal sequences relate to the amino acids; while sonatas, symphonies, and other traditional compositional forms (more difficult to digest, analytically and emotionally) relate to the complex proteins.

Speaking from my own experience, as well as the experience of thousands of others, the key principle may be summarized as follows. *The body is not necessarily impressed by complexity.* A balanced diet most likely would include nourishment from many sources.

Sound Addiction

One of the problems with much of rock and pop music is its standard rhythm, what is called the "stopped-anapestic rhythm"—a "short-short-long-pause" pattern. This stopped-anapestic rhythm tends to confuse the body and weaken the muscles. Among hundreds of persons tested by behavioral kinesiologist Dr. John Diamond, 90 percent registered an almost instantaneous loss of two-thirds of their muscle strength when they heard this beat. Interestingly, this often happens even when the listener likes the music.

The rhythm of much rock music may tend to override the more subtle signals of the body's own communication system. The end result is that the body's system is confused, the heart's response is irregular, and the body gets weakened.

However, the body soon adapts to the stimuli by what has been called the "general adaptation syndrome." This syndrome was first described by Hans Selye, the world-famous researcher on stress. The reason that you are not excessively weakened by listening to rock music with a stopped-anapestic beat is that your body adapts to it.

But this doesn't mean that this beat is now good nourishment for the body or that no harmful effects may come from it. It means merely that the body is somehow masking the rhythm's effect much as it masks its response to unhealthy foods.

That the body possesses an incredible capacity to adapt to less-than-ideal stimuli is not without a price. Just as people who continue to eat junk food soon become conditioned and even addicted to these harmful substances, so people who continue to listen to music that weakens them and confuses their inner natural pulse soon become conditioned and perhaps addicted to this music.

Through addiction, that which is bad for us soon becomes that which we need to carry on. Sound addiction and rhythm addiction are very much like nicotine addiction, sugar addiction, chocolate addiction, caffeine addiction, or addiction to any other drug.

We are not suggesting that people should not listen to or dance to rock and disco music. However, we are saying that people should be aware of music's powerful effect on their health.

Some rhythms seem to be better for the body than others. Pay attention to what your body is telling you, then make informed choices.

Rhythm and movement are the essence of life. Experiencing the rhythm of breathing and moving can be invaluable for getting in touch with ourselves and others. It's also a great deal of fun.

Developing Muscle Coordination

Establishing muscle coordination in children or reestablishing it in older people can be aided by the rhythm in music. Therapeutically, it is known that individuals gain muscular coordination and improved mental coordination when they play musical instruments or listen to rhythmic music.

Dr. E. Bright, in his book *Music and Geriatric Care*, describes how music therapists often conduct sessions in convalescent homes, having senior citizens tap out rhythms or play along on musical instruments, thus gaining control of their motor skills.

When you dance, exercise, or simply tap your fingers to your favorite music, learn to enjoy the variety of subtle movements of which your body is capable. Learn to "feel the beat" without industrial-strength volume. Notice how your body responds to different rhythms, such as 4/4, 6/8, 3/4, 2/4, and even tempo-less music.

Making Music

One of the best ways to have the sound that you want around you is to produce it yourself—with your voice, with a musical instrument, or both.

In this process, we are not talking about the discipline of practicing a musical instrument, but time spent producing music purely for the body's sound nourishment. We are talking about sound and music made spontaneously, and consumed as effortlessly as food is chewed and swallowed. We are talking about times when people spontaneously and often unconsciously nourish themselves with sound and rhythm by whistling, humming, singing, or tapping their toes and fingers. Similar nourishment happens when people get together to sing or to improvise on musical instruments.

Making music creates vibrations and brings sound into the world. When your music has the ability to help yourself or other people relax and get well, it is a gift to the planet.

Groaning and sighing can also be done in ways that are relaxing and promote healing, though few people are aware of this. Two other forms of producing human sound deserve mention. The first is chanting, which induces relaxation and promotes harmony in the body. (Chanting is discussed in Part III, Sound Spirit.) The second is toning.

Toning

We express ourselves with words and sounds. Beneath these words are the vibrations of the tone upon which they travel. Tone is an underlying force operating in our lives. It is the voice, not only of our thoughts, but primarily of our physical body. (For a more detailed discussion, see Laurel Elizabeth Keyes's book *Toning: The Creative Power of the Voice.*)

To do toning, stand comfortably erect and let your body sway as a flower on its stalk in a breeze. Relax your jaw so that your teeth are slightly parted.

Let sound come up from your feet, not down from your mind. Begin with an audible groan, such as "ohhh" or "ahhh," and let it give you a feeling of release, of emptying out, of resting.

Let your body groan as long as it likes, until the tones your body makes surface spontaneously.

Let the toning session last ten minutes or an hour—until the body feels cleansed and nourished and a *sigh is released*. The sigh lets you know that the body-voice is satisfied.

It is hard to describe scientifically what happens during toning. When you do it, you know that you feel good, as though something important inside you has been accomplished. Perhaps it is that the whole person has been brought into harmony once again.

Making Silence

John Cage, a composer of avant-garde music, was one of the first composers to become interested in the relationship between music and Zen philosophy and meditation.

One of his best-known performances—worthy of a Zen master confronting his students with a paradoxical koan—consisted of giving a very formal piano recital in full evening dress, complete with an assistant to turn the pages of the musical score, in which the score consisted entirely of rests.

Although his music, or lack of it, during that silent performance was not what most people would describe as "meditative," his humor and concepts of music and silence helped create a breakthrough in our cultural awareness of sound.

The point of Cage's silent concert wasn't merely to get away with murder in the somewhat eccentric world of avant-garde music. He was announcing that he had discovered and wanted to share a meditative process of listening to silence.

Listening to Silence

This process is simple. Close your eyes and allow your ears to resonate with whatever sounds might be happening in the environment. There is no need to name or identify the sounds, as one might do when normally listening to music. Simply acknowledge the fact that the sounds are touching you.

After a while, you learn to hear sounds emerging from the emptiness of silence. Thus you become an "ear-witness" to the continual beginnings of the universe.

In focusing on silence, composer John Cage called our attention to the multifaceted sonic landscape or soundscape. Using techniques for listening to silence, he hoped to help open the ears—and minds—of the musically educated, and get us all to be conscious of the sounds around us.

Ear Cleaning Exercises

R. Murray Schafer, in *The Tuning of the World*, suggests that most people need what he calls an "ear cleaning" program. It's really "mind-cleaning." In the spirit of John Cage, Schafer wants us to begin hearing consciously and clearly sounds with which we think we are familiar.

One exercise he suggests is to imitate with your voice different nuances of a similar sound. For example, imitate with your voice the sound of a shovel digging into sand, then into gravel, then into clay, then into snow. Only a person who has consciously heard those sounds and recognized their differences will be able to carry out the exercise.

The point of the exercise is not to become a shovel imitator, but one who realizes that there is more to the art of listening and hearing than one might have thought.

An Environmental Composition

As you listen to the world around you, become aware of the wide variety of sounds in the environment, without making a judgment about any of them. After listening for a while, notice how the many sounds tend to relate to each other, how they fit together as part of a large orchestra—a symphony of life, as it were.

For example, notice how birds sing in tune with each other and establish certain rhythms. In this context, even the passing jet plane overhead may come in perfectly on cue.

Speaking from my own experience, I am always intrigued at the non-stop call-and-response performance in nature between birds, insects, frogs, and other nature sounds. Not only that, but they *love* having an audience. With aid of a simple tape recorder to document the "sound evidence," I have proven to many a doubting Thomas that birds come closer and increase their singing when you pay attention. If you travel, you will discover that the environmental composition is different in different areas of the country.

Advanced "environmental composers" enjoy shifting from passive to active mode. Try joining in the environmental performance with your voice or a musical instrument, when appropriate. At first, birds and other animals may be a bit surprised, but soon they will welcome your input. This is especially true if you have a mockingbird tune into your song. The bird may join you in an inter-species jam session.

Summary

In twentieth-century society, the noise level is such that it keeps knocking our bodies out of tune and out of their natural rhythms. This ever-increasing assault of sound upon our ears, minds and bodies adds to the stress load of civilized beings trying to live in a highly complex environment.

This load of noise must be decreased. But decreasing it is not enough, just as it is not enough to stop eating junk food.

The goal is to provide ourselves with a healthy diet, both of food and sound.

Chapter 8

SOUND SYSTEM

From Gill to Ear

"Examine the workings of the human ear," says George Leonard in his book *The Silent Pulse*, "and you might think that there would be some simpler way to devise an organ of hearing. But the ear evolved from the gill, and its strange mechanisms were built upon an organ designed for something entirely different. The levers and pivots that translate the vibrations of the eardrum into the inner ear, as a matter of fact, look like one of those arrangements in the old Rube Goldberg cartoons, and yet they are marvelously sensitive."

The human ear is a technically remarkable instrument. To duplicate the 400,000 separate sounds that this organ can hear, a sophisticated audio engineer would have to construct a highly complex sound system in a space smaller than the size of an ice cube.

The Human Sound System

To appreciate what the ear does for us simply as an auditory organ, let us follow some steps in the process of hearing.

We are all familiar with the first steps. A sound is made in the outer environment—a voice, a bell, a car motor. Its vibrations emanate and are gathered by the external earlobes and ear. They are funneled down to the eardrum, and from there to the conductive mechanisms in the middle ear.

Inside the middle ear's air-filled chamber, a chain of three of the smallest bones in the body, called ossicles, pick up these vibrations and transfer them to the inner ear. While the faintest audible sound (1 dBA) moves the eardrum back and forth only 40 billionths of an inch, the lever action of these tiny bones translates this pressure, twenty-two times greater, onto the fluid of the inner ear. And here, in the cochlea, the first mysteries of hearing begin.

The cochlea, a fluid-filled snail-shaped coil, which may be described as a complex hydraulic system of fluid in motion, houses the sense receptors for hearing. Tiny hairs of different lengths—about 24,000 of them, arrayed like the strings on a harp—are connected to the receptor cells. A tone transmitted from the eardrum to the cochlea causes vibrations in the cochlear fluid. Hairs resonant to that tone will vibrate sympathetically.

The mechanical vibration of those hairs mysteriously triggers an electrical response in the receptor nerve cells to which they are attached. These receptor cells also seem to respond to the pressure of the standing sound waves in the cochlear fluid. Researchers are still asking what the exact molecular mechanism might be whereby a mechanical movement in the hair changes the electrical properties of the receptor cell.

We do know that receptor cells send appropriate messages to the brain. Within the brain the auditory signal, with potential connection to more than 600,000 cells, spreads around a complex circuitry with numerous loops and signal dampers. This marvelous process allows you, for example, to identify your child's voice among many voices in a noisy crowd.

The ear is very discriminating. With vision, we see the blend of three different pigments as a single color. The ear, however, can not only hear a trio of musicians as a single unified sound, *but can also discriminate the sounds of the individual instruments*.

Usually, when we use the words "sound system" we are referring to a set of electronic components such as stereo receivers, loudspeakers, turntables, microphones, etc. We can also see how these components are closely related to the human sound system.

Electronic Sound Systems

Sound travels through the air in the form of rapid pressure waves that create an audible vibration. The number of waves, or vibrations, that occur per second is described in cycles per second, or hertz.

The limits of human hearing in the low-frequency range occur at about 20 hertz, in the upper range at about 20,000 hertz.

When a sound is in the audible range, but is not able to be heard, we need to amplify the sound. To do this we change the sound energy into a more manageable form, usually from acoustic vibrations into electrical signals.

A *transducer* is a device that changes energy from one form to another. A microphone is one example of a transducer which converts sound energy produced by a voice or an instrument into electrical energy. A phonograph cartridge also acts as a transducer, converting the physical vibrations picked up by the stylus in the grooves of the record into an electrical signal.

In both cases, vibrations in the air have been transformed into rapid electrical changes in a wire. These electrical signals may be easily amplified in a power amplifier, and then converted back into sound energy for human hearing through a loudspeaker, which is also a transducer.

High Volumes

However, amplifiers can be used to magnify sound out of all proportion. Some powerful home sound systems come equipped with such high wattage that the decibel level in the room reaches the threshold of pain when the volume is turned up.

Amplifiers with high wattage are very much in evidence in discos and school dances. Because of the danger to the human ear, Maryland State officials require that at school dances, the volume of the music be limited to a maximum of 90 dBA. When the sound meter reads above 90 dBA, the volume of the music at the dance must be turned down.

A Subtle Danger

More subtly dangerous in this regard are miniature headsets, frequently used with today's personal stereo systems. Those who listen to radio or cassettes using miniature headsets with volume turned high—their eardrums only an inch or so from the sound source—may be experiencing the music at a level dangerous to the auditory mechanism.

With personal headphones, you can be exposed to decibel levels well in excess of 100 dBA without even disturbing anybody else. The problem, however, is not with *using* the technology, but in *abusing* it.

Because of this, we feel that manufacturers should be required to educate consumers about sound health and spell out in warnings on the package, just as is done with cigarettes and certain diet sodas. It is important for consumers to be aware of the potential damage that may result from improper use of this or that piece of sound equipment.

People cannot be stopped from misusing sound, just as they cannot be stopped from using cigarettes, alcohol, and diet soft drinks. But at least we can educate them about the harm they may unwittingly be doing to themselves.

Sound Problems

Physical sound translates into the psychological experience of hearing through a series of acoustical events from the ear to the brain. Damage or blockage to any of the auditory structures along this path may distort or hinder the perception of the original sound. This often results in communication problems. Thus people with hearing problems often have difficulty understanding conversation, even with increased volume.

Such problems come from one of four sources. Hearing difficulty may be (1) *conductive*, a hearing impairment in the outer or middle ear; (2) *sensorineural*, a hearing impairment that stems from damage to the inner ear, the cochlea, or the neural fibers; (3) *mixed*, an impairment that is both conductive and sensorineural; or (4) *central*, a problem referring to auditory pathways in the brain which might affect the capacity to understand spoken language.

Acquired Hearing Impairment

Although hearing impairment can be congenital—received by genetic inheritance—most sensorineural hearing problems are acquired. Acquired hearing impairments may take the following forms.

Ototoxic drugs prescribed for life-threatening illness may cause immediate or progressive damage to the inner ear. Neomycin, kanamycin, gentamycin, streptomycin, thalidomide, salicylates, chloroquinine, and quinine are examples of drugs that may cause cochlear or vestibular damage. Whenever a prescribed drug affects your hearing (e.g., by lowering your threshold or by creating a ringing in your ears), notify your doctor so that he or she may alter the dosage or change the drug to prevent hearing impairment.

Viral and bacterial illness such as mumps, meningitis, and encephalitis, as well as rubella contracted by expectant mothers, have been shown to be related to hearing impairment in the child.

Tumors near the eighth nerve (auditory nerve) may not only affect the hearing and vestibular systems, but could have life-threatening implications.

Meniere's disease is characterized by fluctuating loss of hearing, dizziness, and ringing in the ears (tinnitus). Some possible causes of Meniere's disease include allergy, hypothyroidism, and diabetes.

Vascular incidents related to hypertension, heart disease, or other vascular problems may alter blood flow to the inner ear, causing cochlear structures to be deprived of needed oxygen. There is an extensive network of blood vessels located in and around the auditory system. As the blood flow is reduced, so is the supply of oxygen.

Auditory Trauma

In our society, however, the most pervasive cause of sensorineural hearing impairment is *trauma*. While trauma to the ear may happen in an accident in which the skull is damaged and the cochlea fractured, trauma is most often a result of excessively loud noise.

This trauma, usually causing sensory and neural damage within the cochlea, results in a permanent hearing loss. While sensori-neural hearing impairment cannot currently be reversed either medically or surgically, hearing aids can prove quite helpful.

Hearing Tests

When people take steps to deal with hearing loss, they usually begin by entering the world of audiological management. The first visit to an audiologist usually begins with a battery of tests. One of the first tests for suspected hearing loss is the *pure tone test*, which measures the degree of hearing loss. It is measured in relation to a defined norm called "normal hearing."

The healthy ear is able to perceive tones of sound across a wide range of sound frequencies (125–8000 cycles per second) within an intensity (or loudness) range of 0–20 dBA. If higher volume is required just to detect a particular tone, such persons are defined as having a hearing loss. The degree of loss is described on a scale from mild to profound. From *Noise Around Our Homes*, an EPA pamphlet:

Degree of Hearing Impairment	Volume Required in Order to Detect Sound
Mild	20–40 dBA
Moderate	41–55 dBA
Moderately severe	56–70 dBA
Severe	71–90 dBA
Profound	90–plus dBA

An *audiogram* plots hearing thresholds for each ear along a wide range of frequencies. Hearing loss from excessive and loud noises unusually begins with higher frequencies. In practical terms, this means people would have trouble hearing consonants in human speech, although they would still hear vowel sounds, since these normally occur at much lower frequencies. They would, for example, have difficulty distinguishing between words like *bike*, *strike*, and *pike* or *cat*, *bat*, and *pat*. It's easy to see why communication begins to suffer when hearing loss does.

When the Sound System Doesn't Work

Part of the insidious nature of hearing loss is that it usually occurs progressively over a long period of time.

Sometimes months or years pass before a hearing problem is noticed, especially if the deficiency is only in a certain frequency range.

For example, hearing loss in the range of 500 cycles per second results in poor perception of voiceless consonants that are easily confused with one another, such as *m* and *n* or *p*, *b*, and *v*. Such a loss prevents children from learning easily and, as Dr. Bernard suggested in an article in *Brain-Mind Bulletin*, January 24, 1983, hearing deficits in the 500 cycles per second area may be the source of confusion that fosters dyslexia. Dr. Bernard reported that many dyslexics have selective hearing loss in frequencies corresponding to specific phonemes, the sounds which serve as the building blocks of language.

In adults, a hearing loss in the 500 cycles per second range often gets people—both the afflicted one and those listening—irritated, confused, and angry because of the miscommunication that so frequently happens as a result of the hearing deficiency.

In the same issue of *Brain-Mind Bulletin*, according to French physician Alfred Tomatis, a hearing defect in any portion of the audible frequency spectrum produces specific problems. For example, hearing loss between 500 and 1000 cycles per second makes it impossible for a person truly to appreciate music. Defects in the 1000 to 2000 cycles per second range prevent one from singing in tune. Defects above 2000 cycles per second preclude hearing the harmonics and other tonal qualities that make the human voice pleasant and melodious.

Tinnitus

Tinnitus sufferers hear a constant buzzing, hissing, or ringing in the ears, and never know stillness and quiet. There is usually no hearing loss.

Tinnitus may be caused by ototoxic drugs. "Almost anyone can produce a ringing in the ears just by drinking enough cups of coffee, which might be five or fifteen," says Los Angeles tinnitus expert Dr. Jack Pulec. Tinnitus may also be produced by a tumor on the acoustic nerve. One of the most common causes of tinnitus is traumatic, loud noise.

Soldiers in World War II who stood near loud artillery being fired in battle report tinnitus from time to time as long as forty years afterward. Today, industrial noises tend to make tinnitus the most common ear complaint.

Dr. Maurice Miller, New York University professor of audiology, says that tinnitus sufferers can be treated usually either by medication to increase the blood supply to the inner ear, with a hearing aid, or with a tinnitus-masker.

According to Dr. Miller, the tinnitus masker, though theoretically very promising, has provided a workable solution only for a very small minority of patients. A fully acceptable solution to tinnitus has yet to be found.

Richard Carmen is a leading audiologist and a pioneer in the treatment of tinnitus. In his landmark book *Positive Solutions to Hearing Loss*, he demonstrates the vital connections between poor health and hearing loss. He points out that the ear problems are merely local manifestations of systemic disease.

For instance, the brain is 2% of total body weight, yet it requires 25 percent of all its energy. The brain requires 30 percent more glucose (blood sugar) than other parts of the body, 30 percent more oxygen, and equally large amounts of all other nutrients. If the brain is starved, we begin to develop various types of mental and neurological impairments.

The human body has two arteries that relate to the ear: the coronary artery, which supplies the heart, and the otic artery, which supplies nutrition and oxygen to the internal ear. If the otic artery becomes impaired because of decreased circulation of blood to the head, there is a relative stagnation of lymphatic fluids in the internal ear, which gives rise to a whole host of problems.

The only nutrition the inner ear receives comes by way of the blood. Therefore, if blood circulation is impaired by decreased quantity of flow or diminished quality of nutrients in the blood (e.g., less oxygen, fewer vitamins) tinnitus, hearing loss, and balance problems could result.

Carmen's work provides valuable information to enable us to make a sound choice with respect to conserving, nourishing, and preserving our hearing—our marvelous human sound systems. He includes pertinent charts and lists of foods that cause headaches and associated hearing disorders. And, most important, his research demonstrates that tinnitus is as frequently a result of food allergies as exposure to loud noises.

"In summary," concludes Carmen, "because Meniere's disease, hypoglycemia, diabetes, tinnitus, hearing loss, arteriosclerosis, atherosclerosis and heart disease all respond remarkably well to improvements in diet, including the elimination of certain foods, the research strongly suggests a need to carefully examine our food intake."

Research in Finland has shown that diet also has an effect on ear health. A diet high in saturated fat, which usually raises cholestrol levels and increases the likelihood of heart disease, is also instrumental in hearing loss.

Apparently, the same diet that keeps coronary arteries open may be responsible for keeping open the tiny vessels in the ear. Since the inner ear depends on a fresh flow of blood for the nutrients to keep it functioning well, it's easy to guess why arteries constricted by cholesterol can affect hearing.

Ear Care

When was the last time you had an ear check-up? Most of us never give our hearing a second thought. We take our ears for granted except when they hurt.

Most people think that hearing problems are rare, but the fact is that *more people suffer from hearing impairment than from heart disease, cancer, blindness, tuberculosis, multiple sclerosis, and kidney disease combined.*

There are probably two major reasons we don't pay attention to hearing problems. The first is that hearing loss usually comes on gradually, and the second is that almost no hearing impairment is fatal.

How can you tell if you have a hearing problem? Try answering the following questions:

- Do you frequently have to turn up the television volume?
- Do you find yourself often asking people to repeat what they say to you (not because you weren't paying attention, but because you weren't sure you caught their words)?
- Do you miss parts of sentences or words?
- Do you find it almost impossible to distinguish the words of an individual when you are in a noisy crowd?

If you answer affirmatively to any of these questions, it's possible that you have a hearing disorder. But only an ear specialist can tell you for sure by using some of the hearing tests mentioned above.

Protecting Your Ears

If you hear *ringing, buzzing*, or *roaring* in your ears after an extended exposure to noise, it may indicate damage to hair cells in the cochlea. The obvious and best solution is to avoid such noise.

If you experience *diminished hearing* sensitivity after an exposure to loud noise, that's a sign of a hazardous exposure, even if the loss seems to disappear after resting. Again, avoid such noise.

If you can't avoid such noises, take the precaution of wearing some ear protectors. Earmuff-type protectors work very well, but most people find them uncomfortable and won't wear them. Cotton plugs are comfortable and may keep out the wind, but they offer little protection from noise.

Darrell E. Rose, Ph.D., head of audiology at the Mayo Clinic in Rochester, Minnesota, recommends soft foam plugs. "The foam is rolled between the fingers and thumb until it is small enough to insert in the ear; it conforms comfortably to the shape of the ear canal." Plugs are inexpensive, not noticeable, can be work repeatedly, and are very effective noise reducers.

Other authorities recommend the sort of ear plug that is sold to those who shoot firearms recreationally. These devices reduce the sudden impact of the gun blast, and are also quite useful against rock bands and discos.

Earwax

It is also possible that hearing loss can occur when ears are cleaned improperly. This happens when people use cotton-tipped swabs deep in the ear, intending to clean their ears of wax buildup. Instead, they often push the wax in even further, causing impaction.

Normally, claim ear specialists, the waxy buildup in your ears works itself out in several ways. The action of the jawbone while chewing will often dislodge any earwax. Also, little hairs in the ear canal help move the wax outward to the ear opening where it can be collected easily with a swab.

The big fear among specialists is going in too far with a cotton swab, explains Dr. Peggy Williams, an audiologist. "One little slip and you may puncture the ear drum and possibly dislodge the ossicles."

When wax builds up in your ear, most experts recommend having a doctor flush the wax out with warm water using a special syringe. There are over-the-counter earwax softeners that work, but experts recommend against using them too often; most of them are acidic and can eat away the tender skin of the ear.

Ear Appreciation

We would like people to have a greater appreciation for their ears and the marvelous mechanism that allows them to communicate with those they love. We want people to enjoy the wonderful sounds that are available to them.

Helen Keller once said, "Blindness separates people from things, deafness separates them from other people."

PART TWO

Sound Mind

Chapter 9

SOUND PSYCHOLOGY

Sounds and Psychology

Studies of how noise affects the hearing mechanism and other aspects of physical health have been going on for some time. Researchers are also studying how sound and noise affect people psychologically.

Even if noise or certain sounds are not producing a physically damaging effect, could they still be negatively affecting behavior, emotions, thinking, learning, creativity, imagination, and other psychological processes?

The answer seems to be yes.

Hearing is a complex process. The ear's morphology, its neural connections with the brain, and the autonomic nervous system's reactions to sounds are only a few of the components in what we refer to as hearing.

Sounds also usually arouse feelings and imagery in the hearer and evoke a wide variety of responses, such as fear, familiarity, memories, angers, worry, and love. Think of the fear induced by hearing strange sounds in the house during the middle of the night. Or recall the experience of relief when someone you love has been driving home in a severe storm and you finally hear the familiar sound of the car pulling into the driveway.

Sound and Noise

To understand these findings, it is important to differentiate *psychologically* between sound and noise.

For the physicist, sound results from changes in air pressure that are detected by the ears. Sound is treated as a physical reality. In contrast, noise is a psychological term. It refers to unpleasant, unwanted, or intolerable sounds. Sound volume may be measured on a decibel meter, but noise is measured by the listener.

Loud sounds are not always perceived as noise. Certain loud sounds, such as music at a rock concert or cheering at a sports event, may be very desirable and welcome to people who are happy to be there.

In contrast, noise need not always be loud. Certain soft sounds, such as people whispering behind you during a play or a film, may be a noisy intrusion.

Attitudes and beliefs about certain noises and their sources are often of equal or greater importanct to people than the physical intensity of the sound. Thus complaints about noise are not usually accurate indicators of the volume of sound measured in decibels.

Once a loud sound is perceived as an uninvited noise—the neighbors playing music you don't like on their stereo, for example—annoyance increases as the volume of the sound is increased. But when the same sound is perceived as desirable and welcome—you playing music you like on your own stereo—psychological enjoyment seems to increase as the volume is increased.

In some extreme cases, such as discos and rock concerts, even when the volume reaches a level painful to the physical system, the sound may be perceived as pleasurable. The difference between pain and pleasure becomes blurred.

Attitudes Toward Noise

One of the first general findings of noise research concerns people who have some control over or investment in their acoustical environment.

When people believe that traffic noise affects them economically, they feel different levels of annoyance, depending on their beliefs. In Pennsylvania, people living near a new limited-access highway were asked their feelings about the new highway. Those who believed it would adversely affect the value of their property were more annoyed by the noise than were those who believed it would increase their property value.

This relationship between property values and annoyance at traffic noise from the new highway remained constant, no matter how far people lived from the highway.

When people believed that the road brought them other benefits, such as more jobs and easier access to shopping centers, churches, and other services, they were less annoyed by the traffic noise than those who believed differently. Traffic noise annoyance was found to be unaffected by age, education, and income.

As researcher Sheldon Cohen, professor of psychology at the University of Oregon, sums it up in *Behavior, Health, and Environmental Stress* (1982), "It appears that the meaning of a noise for a particular respondent is crucial to his or her perception of it."

Noise and Mental Illness

"If noise causes irritation and frustrations," says Dr. Cohen, "it seems plausible that prolonged exposure can cause or aggravate mental illness."

Psychiatrist Alex Tarnopolsky's research at the Institute of Psychiatry in London clearly suggests that noise not only may increase the number of psychiatric cases, it may aggravate the problems of those already suffering from psychological problems.

Along these lines, Cohen and his colleagues have shown that children living near Los Angeles International Airport did not perform as well on difficult and complex tasks compared to similar children in quiet areas of Los Angeles. They were also more likely to give up in discouragement.

While Cohen's research was carried out with children, the implication is that loud noise may adversely influence anyone's ability to learn, to utilize learned skills, to concentrate, and to stick to a task.

Noise and Antisocial Behavior

Another psychological effect of noise is that it tends to make people *antisocial*.

In one experiment, reported by Sheldon Cohen in *Psychology Today* (1981), a researcher whose arm was in a cast dropped a pile of books and papers on the sidewalk just as pedestrians were walking by. The researcher would begin picking them up, looking helpless and needing assistance. Another researcher was operating behind a power lawn mower on the grass several feet away.

When the lawn mower was silent, 80 percent of passers-by stopped to help pick up the books and papers. But when the mower was on, only 15 percent stopped.

Noise also psychologically affects people by making them less sympathetic. Cohen (1981) reported that students in a psychological experiment were asked to evaluate resumes from job applicants and recommend starting weekly salaries for each. Student evaluators in a quiet room recommended an average monthly salary of $1000 for the job applicants, while student evaluators in a noisy office (70 to 80 dBA) recommended average salaries of $900 or less.

Noise and Aggression

Noise has a clear effect on aggression, a common expression of anger. Laboratory studies seem to indicate that while loud noise itself may not be sufficient to cause aggression, noise heightens a predisposition to anger or to act aggressively.

In everyday life, most of us can recall extreme reactions to noise—most notably, expressing a wish to strangle or kill the noise-maker.

Music and Emotions

It has long been recognized that certain rhythms and harmonies can affect our emotions, sometimes intensifying them, sometimes transforming them. Fast parade marches are designed to produce energy, excitement, and forward movement, while slow funeral music tends to evoke sadness, solemnity, and dignity.

Traditionally, music researchers have associated major modes with happiness and minor modes with sadness. But we now realize that such generalizations are much too simplistic. For example, many joyful gypsy dances are written in a minor mode. Likewise, many upbeat and uplifting jazz tunes are written in dorian (minor) mode.

On the other hand, many country and western songs are written in major modes, and yet produce sad emotions in the listener.

Clearly, it's not just the notes, but what one *does* with the notes.

Melodic direction is another variable that influences mood. Melodies that favor ascending patterns tend to generate emotional responses different from melodies with descending patterns. The ancient Greeks, for example, sang their scales in descending fashion. In contemporary practice, we sing them in ascending fashion. The emotional effect is different in each case.

An Exercise

As a simple exercise, sing a steadily ascending glissando on the vowel sound "O"—that is, sing "Oh-h-h-h," sliding like a siren up the scale.

Then reverse the process, singing "Oh-h-h-h," sliding down the scale.

Notice in each instance how you feel, both physically and emotionally. Do you notice the difference?

Repeat the procedure once more, this time using the sound "Ah," and observe your emotional responses.

The point of this is to show that very simple musical elements, such as the direction and vowel sound (tone), can often produce specific emotional effects.

Eliciting Emotional Response with Music

When we examine longer musical selections, the task of identifying their emotional effects proves to be much more complicated.

In 1937, in a pioneering article in *The American Journal of Psychology*, Kate Hevner suggested the model of an eight-spoked wheel in order to define the spectrum of affective responses to poetry and music. The eight elements are (1) solemn and sacred, (2) sad and doleful, (3) tender and sentimental, (4) quiet and soothing, (5) sprightly and playful, (6) gay and happy, (7) exhilarated and exciting, (8) vigorous and majestic.

Hevner felt that responses to poetry or to musical selections could be classified in one or other of the eight general categories of her mood wheel.

In 1970 music therapist Dr. Helen Bonny chose twenty-three pieces (popular, classic, operatic, folk, jazz) that seemed to her to have well-integrated and clearly focused moods. Yet when experimental subjects listened to the selections and were asked to assign each to one of Hevner's eight mood categories, they agreed on only seven or eight selections, which was only about 30 percent of the selections.

Clearly, music has a strong emotional impact on listeners—but that impact is not generally specifically predictable, except in a small number of cases!

However, as will become clear in the next chapter, the nonspecificity of the emotions elicited by certain selections may prove helpful to the music therapist. This is especially true in approaches to therapy that utilize imaginative responses to the emotional quality of the music.

Music in the Marketplace

A good deal of research has been done to show how music affects performance in such fields as industry, education, and sports.

The use of music in industry began in earnest around 1940, although studies were begun in the 1930s. The January 1943 issue of *Mechanical Engineering* printed Professor Burris-Meyer's famous speech about background music. He reported controlled studies showing that music in industrial settings led to increased productivity and reduction in absenteeism. This speech gave great impetus to the use of background music in the workplace.

However, we now know that the good results Burris-Meyer reported were due only in part to the music. Another significant variable contributing to results was what is known as the Hawthorne effect. This phenomenon describes how, in a boring, monotonous work situation, the addition of any outside stimulus creates a positive effect on the workers.

The use of background music, pioneered by a company whose name—Muzak—is now a generic, has become omnipresent in public establishments. Each day, it is said that 60 million people around the world listen to Muzak. Add to that the millions surrounded by the sounds of other background music companies and radio stations. That's a lot of people.

And almost all of these people, who usually must listen to the music programming whether they like it or not, are affected psychologically as well as physiologically. We are now assaulted in elevators, restaurants, supermarkets, department stores, banks, mortuaries, and other unlikely places.

Programming Emotions

The programming format of background-music companies is usually quite rigid, formalized, and manipulative. Programming experts create musical scenarios to exact specifications.

According to a Muzak in-house publication entitled *Environs* (1972), "program specialists . . . assign values to the elements in a musical recording, i.e., tempo (number of beats per minute); rhythm (waltz, fox trot, march); instrumentation (brass, woodwinds, strings); and orchestra size (five piece combo, thirty piece symphony, etc.)." There are few soloists, either vocal or instrumental. Musical selections are included in a program only if they measure up to the formula.

Programs are psychologically designed to give a sense that time is dynamically and significantly moving forward. "Each fifteen-minute segment of Muzak contains a rising stimulus which provides a logical sense of forward movement," is the way the promotional literature puts it. "This affects boredom or monotony and fatigue." The literature seems to ignore the reality that many listeners are bored—or worse—by their selections.

Music Working Psychologically

There is no doubt, psychologically, that music can serve to aid employee alertness and productivity, especially in boring and repetitive jobs. Employee productivity can be manipulated (speeded up or slowed down) by the music programmers. So, too, can people's purchasing habits and eating habits be affected by music programmed in supermarkets, department stores, and restaurants.

Here's another simple bit of research that you can do on your own. The next time that you go to a sit-down format, fast-food establishment, notice if the mouths of your fellow diners are chewing in synchronization to the beat of the background music. Ask them if they like the music, and they will usually reply, "What music?"

Although "Eat to the Beat" was a big hit in the early 1980s, conceptually it remains on the all-time fast food hit parade. It's no secret that the management is interesting in moving meat—theirs, as well as yours—in and out of their establishment.

At a shopping mall with recently installed background music, Dr. Murray Schafer discovered that while only 25 percent of the shoppers thought they spent more money as a result of the background music, 60 percent of the shopkeepers thought they did! We get the message, even if we can't "name that tune!"

Sound and Music Working at an Unconscious Level

For years, Madison Avenue has used subliminal artwork in advertising. Dr. Wilson Brian Key has documented this media assault on our conscious and unconscious minds in his landmark book *Subliminal Seduction*. Now it appears that the areas of unconscious manipulation has expanded to include sound as well as print.

In 1979, *The New York Times* and *The Wall Street Journal* reported that Dr. Hal Becker of Tulane University, a pioneer in subliminal sound, had devised a way to disguise verbal commands in background music. Becker's research opened up a Pandora's box of subliminal suggestions using sound.

In essence, this technique deploys the verbal suggestion at a volume so low that the conscious mind cannot perceive it. All that one hears consciously is the music. Meantime, the conscious mind absorbs and responds to the verbal suggestion.

Music and the Subconscious Mind

Up to this point, we've been focusing primarily on the psychological effects of music in the conscious domain. But scientists are discovering the existence of computer-like programs that can access the inner codes of the mind more effectively.

A concert pianist and neuropsychologist at the State Conservatorium of Music in Sydney, Australia, Dr. Manfred Clynes, in his book *Sentics: The Touch of Emotions* (1979), states that it appears that some of these codes are related to rhythm, melody, and intervallic relationships between tonal frequencies (harmony). These codes in the nervous system may influence and condition our response to the emotional and rhythmic qualities of musical expression. Moreover, they may have affected the initial creation of these qualities.

Dr. Clynes says that there are specific forms of emotional expression—called "essentic forms"—that act like keys in a lock, and "activate specific brain processes to which we react." Research suggests that essentic forms have innate meanings that transcend cultural learning and conditioning and are therefore neurologically coded.

This discovery lifts the question of how music communicates and how it changes our moods out of the exclusive province of esthetics or music criticism. The study of the science of "sentics" has profound implications for musicians in the area of interpretation, performance, and composition. We hope that it will help usher in a new golden age of music.

Another piece of the puzzle of how music affects us fell into place when Rupert Sheldrake, a plant physiologist, published his revolutionary theory of evolution in 1981. In *A New Science of Life*, Sheldrake theorizes that the universe functions not so much by immutable laws as by "habits"—patterns that have been created by the repetition of events over time.

According to this hypothesis, organizing fields, called morphogenetic fields, serve as blueprints for form and behavior. In other words, once a pattern of behavior is manifested, it becomes easier for others in that species to perform that same behavior through what is called morphic resonance.

This holds true whether the activity involves a rat learning a maze or a crystal growing in a sealed laboratory jar. It also may relate to the way that we relate to music, in that we may be resonating to the ways that others of our species have responded to music in the past.

Words and Music

The addition of the spoken word to a musical program usually results in the music becoming background to the text. Unfortunately, this also results in a situation in which the analytical left hemisphere of the brain assumes dominance as it "pays attention" to the "message." In this mode, it is easy to consciously resist what is being said.

One of the most popular lines of tapes is of a self-help variety. Such tapes offer to help the listener change a bad habit (like smoking), develop a new one (like good study habits or a better golf stroke), decrease stress (autogenic relaxation), and so on.

Many of these spoken-word cassettes are just that: the spoken word. Narrators speak their piece. No frills. And yet, for many people, they seem to work well.

Psychologist John Adams conducted a study in his clinical practice to see if the addition of music to his spoken relaxation program would enhance its effectiveness. On one side of his tape, he recorded his standard format. On the other side, he recorded the same words, but with the addition of the relaxing soundtrack of *Spectrum Suite* in the background.

He discovered that over 80 percent of his clients preferred the side with music. When given a choice, that was the side that they listened to. And, more important, that was the side that they would listen to over and over.

With the music present, they did not get tired of the words!

Music with Words

If background music can be such a powerful adjunct to the spoken word, what might the effect be if the positions were reversed?

What if the music was in the foreground, and the words were in the background?

Out of such questions came the development of yet another manifestation of psychotechnology. It goes by many names: subliminal suggestion, twilight learning, Threshold Affirmation®, Harmonic Affirmations®, etc.

Basically, each approach aims at creating the ideal blend of music and voice that will deliver the maximum desired result. The approaches vary considerably, both in volume of the spoken word (from loud whispers to virtually inaudible), and in speed of the spoken words (some are speeded up, some are slowed down, some are normal speed). They also vary in the choice of music or white noise (ocean) in the background. Some work with our hearing apparatus in a monophonic mode (as if we had only one ear), while others address the right and left ears independently.

There are satisfied customers for each brand. This makes our role as general theoreticians difficult. We cannot explain why such diverse approaches work. Studies of their relative effectiveness are yet to be done.

It also makes your role as consumer challenging. With so many approaches to choose from, how do you know what will work for you?

You don't. There's no easy answer. Many of the firms offer money-back guarantees. So if you are not satisfied with the quality or the results, you are not penalized for experimenting. You don't have to be stuck with a dud.

Summary

In the past, the predominant research evidence has been collected to show what noise can do to harm your psychological health or how music can be used to manipulate your psychological responses.

In the coming decades, we predict that sound evidence will be collected that will demonstrate what certain types of music can do to promote your psychological health, develop your abilities, and liberate your creativity.

The following chapters will show how music has been used as a helpful tool in developing imagination, fostering learning, and facilitating psychotherapy.

Chapter 10

SOUND IMAGINATION

The Healing Power of Imagery

For thousands of years and throughout many cultures, imagination has been regarded as a powerful agent in the healing process. Unfortunately, this has not been the case in our own time.

But the tide is turning. In recent years, many experimental and clinical studies have shown that mental images can help bring about rapid and far-reaching emotional, psychological, and physiological changes.

In fact, in terms of psychological health, we seem to be in the decade of the imagination. Twenty years ago, imagery and imagination were considered the exclusive domain of the artist, musician, poet, and writer. Imagination was an issue for aesthetics, not psychology.

Currently, interest in the healing capacity of images continues to blossom. In the last few years, in psychological and educational circles, a series of books and articles about imagination have begun appearing. Announcements for nationwide conferences focusing on the imaginal mode of thinking are no longer a surprise in the mail. New professional journals with the terms "imagination" or "imagery" in their titles are being published.

In exploring the healing connection between imagery and music, one place to begin is in the field of music therapy.

Music Therapy

Music therapy is traditionally defined as the systematic application of music by the music therapist to bring about helpful changes in the emotional or physical health of the client.

Music therapists, in private and institutional settings, encourage a variety of musical activities and responses in clients—learning to sing or play a musical instrument, participating in a chorus or instrumental ensemble, moving or drawing to music, and eliciting imagery in response to music. Undergraduate and graduate programs in music therapy, available at many colleges and universities, usually combine academic and clinical training toward the Registered Music Therapist (R.M.T.) degree.

The Journal of Music Therapy, from 1964 to the present, illustrates the areas where music therapy researchers have been exploring the functional uses of sound and music as they affect physiology, behavior, emotions, learning, and the therapeutic process.

Music and the Brain

According to a summary of research edited by M. Critchley and R. A. Henderson called *Music and the Brain: Studies in the Neurology of Music*, at least three neurophysiological processes may be activated in response to music stimuli.

First, because music is nonverbal, it can move through the auditory cortex directly to the center of the emotional responses, presumed to lie in the limbic system. (Traditional verbalizations of the therapist, which may be summary statements that tend to create resistance in the client, usually have their primary effect in the cortical region, especially in the logical and analytic left hemisphere of the brain.)

Second, music may be able to activate the flow of stored memory material across the corpus collosum, so that right and left hemispheres of the brain work in harmony rather than in conflict.

Third, calming and quieting music may well help produce the large molecules called peptides that relieve pain by acting on specific receptors in the brain.

Therapeutically, this means that properly selected music used in a psychotherapeutic session can act almost as a co-therapist by evoking emotional responses, releasing material stored in memory, and relieving certain neurological pain. The music seems able to

influence clients nonverbally in ways not open to the human therapist, who is limited to words.

Imagery, Music, and Emotions

Because music evokes nonverbal, emotional responses, it is
sometimes called the language of the emotions. More important
for the therapist, music seems to evoke meanings, both general and
specific, that were never intended by the composer.

In the eighteenth century, when composer Antonio Vivaldi was
writing *The Four Seasons*, he never expected that one of his listeners in the twentieth century would say, "That music reminds me of
a happy childhood summer that I spent on Uncle Ed's and Aunt
Angie's farm in Indiana."

Music can evoke and sustain such emotional affect, claim music
therapists I. A. Taylor and F. Paperte, writing in the *Journal of
Aesthetics* (1958), by its capacity for "depth provocation."

"Music, because of its abstract nature," they explain, "detours
around the ego and intellectual controls and, contacting the lower
(brain) centers directly, stirs up latent conflicts and emotions
which may be expressed and re-enacted through music."

As aesthetic philosopher Susan Langer pointed out in her semi-
nal book *Philosophy in a New Key* in 1942, music helps us formu-
late and represent our emotions, moods, mental tensions, and
resolutions.

Guided Imagery and Music

One special way that music can be productively used in therapeutic settings is in its capacity to elicity imagery. People have long
known that music stimulates the imagination, but an effective process for doing this was probably first systemmatized by Helen L.
Bonny and Louis M. Savary in 1973, in their book *Music and Your
Mind*.

Based on studies at the Maryland Psychiatric Research Center
in Baltimore and the exploratory work with "guided affective imagery" (without music) of Dr. Hanskarl Leuner in Europe, Dr.

eloped an innovative approach to music-listening called
magery and Music (GIM), which encourages a response
in the form of kinesthetic, visual, and feeling imagery.

onny defines GIM as the conscious use of imagery, which
has been evoked by relaxation and music, to effect self-understanding and personal growth processes in the individual.

Together, Bonny and Savary founded the Institute for Consciousness and Music to carry on continued work in this area. As a
music therapist, Helen Bonny's main interests were psychological
and therapeutic.* She researched music that would provide an appropriate mood structure for exploring conflicted areas of the self,
without limiting the client's flow of imagery. The music, she found,
often opened listeners to a wide variety of other experiences—such
as positive, oceanic, transpersonal, and religious imagery—that
might have life-changing properties.

A variety of ways of therapeutically working with imagery and
symbols surfaces while listening to music. "For those who are seek-
ing to develop new and effective modes of healing," said Helen
Bonny from the therapist's perspective, speaking at the National
Conference of Music Therapists in 1983, "it appears that research
and development in the skillful use of sound through music may
have promise for the healing of people in the future even more effectively than the ancient and traditional patterns of the past. New
insights may allow greater differentiation and control of purpose-
less noise that pollutes body and mind and may promote the sensitive and healing use of sounds that we call music."

An essential skill in the therapeutic use of music is the ability to
tell, in individual cases, which music serves a healing purpose and
which does not. To develop this skill, specialized training in music a
well as in psychology is essential.

Training for therapists who wish to use GIM is provided in in-

---

*Dr. Savary, whose main interests were in facilitating transpersonal and spiritual
growth, chose to develop the guided-imagery-and-music process to evoke meditative, creative, transpersonal, and spiritual states of consciousness. This will be discussed in Part III, Sound Spirit.

ternship programs at the Institute for Consciousness and Music and at certain colleges and universities. Many therapists are now qualified to use GIM as a therapeutic procedure. They are indeed a new breed of therapists.

Images Evoked by Music

In the GIM techniques, the link connecting the therapist and client is found in the series of images reported by the client listening to music. These images become the raw material to be worked with in order to produce therapeutic insight and behavioral change.

Used in a one-to-one relationship with a trained guide, GIM has proved to be a powerful psychological uncovering process. It helps explore levels of consciousness not usually available to normal consciousness, yet relevant to the therapeutic process. The music, in fact, facilitates the process. The musical selections are chosen because of their ability to initiate or continue the listener's mood or experiential state. Various elements of music—instrumental timbre, vocal color, rhythm, harmony, melody, intensity—contribute subtly and powerfully to the listener's mood, emotional involvement, and inner journey.

Although it is important that the client begin the GIM process in a relaxed state of consciousness, the function and objective of the GIM session is not simply to relax the listener. Often, therapeutically, the desire may require the opposite—for example, to evoke strong affect, such as anger. Thus, programming selections for a GIM psychotherapy session involves not only understanding how to match music to the client's generalized mood-state, but also how to recognize the musical qualities that may elicit imagery to foster self-understanding and personal growth in this individual at this moment.

Why Use Music?

How is imagery produced? Can't we generate imagery simply by daydreaming or by consciously using our creative imagination? If so, then why use music to do it?

There are two reasons. First, not everyone can create vivid mental imagery at will. No matter what our natural capacity, research has shown that we tend to generate more imagery, with greater intensity and duration, with music than without.

In 1979, two researchers at Florida State University, Alexandra Quittner and Robert Glueckauf, compared ninety college students in their ability to create inner imagery while listening to music (in this case, *Spectrum Suite*), and while merely relaxed in a silent environment. They found that the average imagery production of the students was significantly higher under the music condition than under the merely relaxed condition. Scores on the Creative Imagination Scale were significantly correlated with the quality and duration of the imagery.

The second reason for using music to facilitate imagery is that specific musical selections tend to elicit certain kinds of imagery. In other words, specific music can help focus and promote a specific therapeutic result.

Music therapists using GIM need to be well-versed in the emotional potentials of certain musical selections. They must also be sensitive enough to choose for the client the right music at the right time. Choosing music for therapeutic intervention is not something that an untrained individual could do for himself or herself at home.

People who are in mental institutions or are working through major personality disorders with a non-music therapist ought not to attempt any form of self-therapy using music.

Therapeutic Music at Home

For most people, however, even without training or the assistance of a music therapist, a simple program of imaging to music may be done while listening to music. Bonny's and Savary's *Music and Your Mind* offers a variety of suggestions for doing this.

Discovering personal meaning in symbolic imagery is a quality some people intuitively possess and a skill that others, usually therapists, spend many hours of study and training to develop. It is not our intention in these pages to teach such skill. Nor do we intend to discuss ways of therapeutically working with the imagery and symbolism that surfaces while listening.

Readers interested in learning to process symbolic imagery may find help in Carl Jung's writings on the "active imagination" such as *Man and His Symbols* or in Mary Watkins's book *Waking Dreams*. The suggestions for using music given in the following pages are not intended for therapeutic work that requires professional help.

A flow of images during relaxation time can enrich you and help the time pass more enjoyably. On the other hand, you may also find it helpful to listen to stimulating and exciting music, and watch the "movies in your mind" unfold. It seems that the flow of images that occurs while listening (and relaxing) can prove therapeutic even if no attempt is made to interpret or find psychological meaning in the images.

The Imagination's Inner Senses

In this chapter, we use the term imagery in a very general sense. Perhaps "inner sensory response" would be more adequate.

The human imagination has within it a complete set of inner senses corresponding to the external senses of sight, sound, smell, taste, and touch. That is, we can see, hear, smell, taste, and touch with our imagination. For example, while you sit at your dinner table you can also imagine yourself at your favorite vacation spot; your imagination's inner senses can recreate the sensory details of that place.

When we use the term "images" or "imagery" in connection with music, we include the inner sensory responses, not only of sight, but of any or all of the senses. The following exercise suggests a way to introduce imaging into your relaxation as you listen. It may be used with a hundred variations, limited only by your naturally creative and fertile imagination.

An Exercise: How to Relax with Inner Imagery

1. Select a time and location when you're not likely to be disturbed, so that you can place your full attention on the soothing and relaxing music you have chosen to play.
2. Take a comfortable position, either sitting or lying down.
3. Close your eyes and take three slow, deep breaths, enough to invite your body to relax and to let it know that may remain relaxed for the length of the music.
4. When you feel relaxed, begin the music. (Some people find it distracting to get up from their comfortable position to turn on the music. If you are one of these, turn on the music immediately after step 1).
5. As the music plays, allow your imagination to visualize pleasant surroundings—a beautiful meadow filled with flowers, a sparkling a bubbly stream, the beach and ocean, or your own favorite scene.
6. Once you have pictured the scene in your mind, encourage your imagination not only to see the scene, but to hear the sounds that are there, to touch things that are there, to taste and smell what is there. Let yourself actively participate in the scene. Interact with the grass, flowers, sand, water, or whatever else appears to be there. In this way, you will spend your time enjoyably in the deeply relaxed state.

Creatively Visualizing What You Really Want

As an alternative to the inner imagery suggested above, you may chose, as the music plays, to visualize something that you want to attain in your life, some result you really want.

You may picture it flowing into your life. Or you may imagine yourself enjoying right now whatever it is that you wish to attain.

For example, you may picture your currently messy desk or closet clean and well-ordered, with everything in place.

Or you may picture yourself freely and honestly relating to someone with whom you are now having difficulty communicating.

Or you may visualize yourself skiing in perfect form on the Swiss Alps, or driving a responsive sports car along a beautiful, winding country road.

"But I Haven't Got a Good Imagination . . ."

Although many people have vivid imaginations and can easily get into imagery while listening to music, there are some who cannot seem to get started. Here are a few observations.

It is possible that you, like 10 to 20 percent of people, are not a visually oriented person. If you are one of these, try focusing instead on tactile or kinesthetic sensations. As the music plays, watch what happens in your body. Do you feel a tingling in your fingertips, a sense of floating, a sense of heat or coolness, a surge of energy? Can you feel the music touch your body? Can you feel it on your face or arms?

Another alternative is to focus on affective or feeling responses, whether or not they are accompanied by imagery. Does the music make you feel peaceful, loving, trusting, calm, at one with yourself and the world?

It is important to realize that there are many ways to listen successfully to relaxing music without having inner visual imagery.

Developing Visual Imaginative Skills

Those who wish to develop visual imaginative skills should begin by focusing on *details*. For example, if you cannot visualize the ocean and beach, can you visualize a pebble or a sea shell? Can you observe its colors and shapes? Can you imaginatively run your finger along its sides and feel its textures? Many people learn to visualize well by starting with little things.

Relaxation and Stress

Relaxing and visualizing with music is not merely a pastime. It has much to do with creating good health.

Research has shown that stress changes the chemistry of the

body in many ways. When you have too much stress, your resistance to disease is lowered. The work of Dr. Hans Selye, Dr. Kenneth Pelletier, Dr. Arthur Gladman, and many others, seems to indicate that almost every disease—from cancer to the common cold—is adversely affected by excessive stress. While some stress is normally beneficial and healthy (physical exercise and mental challenges), the stress referred to here is usually excessive and destructive.

These researchers advocate that people can take action to relieve such stress and thus avoid becoming its victim.

Techniques for relieving stress through music may be done at home, in the office, sometimes even in the car—wherever you find it convenient. As we have seen, the use of soothing and uplifting music connects you to a universal reservoir, which sends messages to your body to relax and allow it to help tune itself.

The mind and imagination, through the creation of inner imagery and other sensory responses, can enhnace this relaxation response. Thus, by enjoying inner imagery, you are promoting your own health and wholeness.

Chapter 11

SOUND EDUCATION

Lobbying for Sound

The National Institutes of Health (NIH) have eleven divisions, among them a National Eye Institute. Conspicuously absent, however, is a National Ear Institute.

When you fill out your federal income tax form, only one disability is mentioned on page one that can be claimed as an exemption; blindness. "That's not because the IRS thinks that blindness is the worst disability," explains Mr. Howard E. Stone, president of Self Help for Hard of Hearing People, Inc., in the Washington, D.C. area. "It's because the blind have been very effective in articulating their problem and acquiring the kind of assistance they need." In other words, the blind have an effective lobby in Congress. The hearing impaired don't.

"The only way for the hearing-impaired to have an effective lobby," Mr. Stone explains, "is to have a healthy and educated constituency. Only then can we move into the area of advocacy."

Education and awareness must come first. No one in Congress, or anywhere else, will understand lobbying for sound health until conscious awareness of the dangers of excessive noise and the tremendous potential for enhancing health through sound and music are in everyone's mind. Americans know little about how sound affects not only their hearing mechanism, but also their general physical and emotional health. How can we help educate people to become aware of their sound environment?

How can sound be used to enhance the process of education and learning in general?

Starting Early

As in most education, so too with sound education: the earlier people learn about it, the better.

A Noise Workbook for elementary school children was prepared by Donna McCord Dickman, Ph.D., sponsored by the EPA. Using crossword puzzles, charts, games, checklists, and things to color, children become aware of how the ear works and how loud noises can cause hearing impairment. After learning how decibels measure noise, the students make a chart with the decibel levels of various noises they hear in everyday life.

The American Speech-Language-Hearing Association (ASHA) and the EPA produce posters and pamphlets encouraging children to become conscious of noise in their lives and to treat their hearing apparatus with care. Materials available for children are mentioned in the section Sound Helps at the end of the book.

Operation Shhh

Self Help for Hard of Hearing People, Inc. (SHHH) is a wonderfully compassionate and creative group of volunteers, most of whom suffer from hearing impairment. They have initiated a program called "Operation Shhh" that teaches young children about noise, and encourages them to take an active role in protecting their hearing.

The part of Operation Shhh that creates the most interest among the children is a traffic light hooked up to a decibel meter. The sound-activated traffic light is usually placed in the school cafeteria or other noisy location, and remains green as long as the noise there remains at an acceptable level. When the yellow light begins flashing, it means the noise is approaching a level which, if sustained, might do damage to hearing. When the light turns red and a buzzer sounds, the noise is definitely dangerous. When the red light goes on, it is a sign for the children to stop talking until the green light goes on again.

"The use of the light system has two purposes," explains Howard

E. Stone, Sr., president of SHHH. "To reduce the actual noise level in the cafeteria, and to create a standard of comparison for the children to begin applying in other situations."

Using a volunteer approach to maintain the student program, the people at SHHH enlist a community service organization to adopt an elementary school and pay for the "traffic light," other printed materials, and the sound awareness posters that go with the program.

Shhherman

The star of Operation Shhh is smiling, lovable Shhherman, a lion that does not roar. Shhherman's picture appears on the series of eight posters intended to make children conscious of noise and hearing.

The creators of this program believe that it will increase awareness about hearing loss among young people, and that young people will carry the message home to their parents and siblings. Speaking of Operation Shhh, Mr. Stone said, "If it preserves the hearing of even one child, it will be a great success."

Teaching children and others about the possible harmful effects of noise on the auditory system and on the human body is only one side of the educational challenge. The other side is to teach people how to use sound and music constructively and creatively to nourish and promote their physical and mental health.

In meeting both these challenges, we have barely begun. But we *have* begun.

Mental Development through Art and Music

For the past decade or so, budget cutters and back-to-basics zealots have been hacking away at "frills" in our schools. Inevitably, art and music are among the first victims.

Important new evidence shows that not only is study of art and music beneficial in itself, but the introduction of these subjects into a school's curriculum causes marked improvement in math, reading, and the sciences. Indeed, some researchers are now suggesting that the absence of art and music programs can retard brain development in children.

Art and music clearly have far more than an enrichment role in the school, because they appear to stimulate a child's natural curiosity and perhaps literally to expand the capacity of the brain. Even more important, they can help children discover their own worth and identity and perhaps even open the gateway to a career.

Music throughout the Curriculum

Up till now, the uses of music in the curriculum have been narrowly focused toward appreciation and factual knowledge. For example, children learn the words and melody to certain patriotic and other traditional American songs; they learn the basics of musical notation—flats, sharps, key signatures, and the rest; they are "exposed" to classical music and to important names in the history of music. But very little emphasis is placed on the students' affective response to music or how their bodies feel when making music or listening to it.

Ideally, *sound and music should be used educationally throughout the curriculum.* Music need not be relegated simply to being a specialty class, but may be used in a much broader, more integrated way: as a tool to promote physical and psychological health; as a tool to combat stress and produce relaxation; as a catalyst for creativity in various subjects in the curriculum; as a setting for deeper concentration during study; as an accelerator for learning language and other skills; as a means to exercise all parts of the brain; and as a source of physical and mental energy.

Music for Relaxation and Learning

Relaxation is especially important in the classroom, both for students and teachers. Researchers have documented that when we become stressed we listen with only half our brains. When students are stressed, they cannot study or comprehend well.*

---

*We have already described ways to use music to help people relax and deal with stress in Part I.

Perhaps if students were more relaxed, they could learn better. If they learned better, they would enjoy school more. If they enjoyed learning, they would tend to become more fully involved in and excited about the learning process. If they became fully involved, learning would become a vital and holistic experience.

And if learning became vital for students, they would then enjoy receiving and sharing the energy that comes from all the learners in the classroom.

Music and Creativity

Music may be used to foster creativity. Appropriate music, simply played in the background, is capable of activating brainwaves in the alpha and theta frequency ranges, which are known to stimulate creativity.

Music selections may be listened to in a relaxed state by students before and during drawing class, creative story-telling periods, writing class, or whenever a child's intuition or imagination needs to be called forth. Teachers who have done so report a marked increase in students' performance from preschool through college.

Music and Imagery in the Classroom

Music and imagery have come to the classroom in some schools. Ann McClure, a professional performer and instructor of music and dance, and an associate at the Institute for Consciousness and Music, has been using music creatively in an optional program in private and public elementary schools for the past few years.

She begins by discussing with students the imagination and the different types of imagery that might occur while listening to music.

Next, she takes students through a series of tension-releasing exercises in order to help them relax. They do the exercises sitting comfortably at their desks or, when possible, lying on a carpeted floor.

When they are relaxed, a narration-plus-music selection is played from a "creative listening" recording. While the music plays, they are told to let the music carry their imaginations wherever it might lead them.

Afterward, they are encouraged to draw with colored crayons some image or scene from their music-listening time. The drawing period is usually followed by a sharing session.

As one teacher observing the process remarked, "The children were deeply engrossed in the entire process. It was as though they had been hungering for such an experience for a long time, and their minds simply devoured it."

Invariably, the children asked for more music and imagery experiences. It seemed when they listened to the music and shared with others what happened, they were discovering a hidden part of themselves.

"I believe my generation grew up without a specific emphasis on self-discovery," explains Ann McClure in *Children's Imagery* (1982). "Creativity was not a primary focus of educators, counselors, or parents. By involving children in the imagery and music process, I have witnessed in them an opening of creative and personality channels which I believe would have traditionally been overlooked."

Music and Movement Exercises

Outside of gym class and random running around during recess periods, elementary school children seldom learn any small-motor and large-motor skills to develop and refine their muscles.

Children may be encouraged to make movements to music. Begin with simple movements of the fingers and arms, such as making lines and circles in the air. Then, standing in one place, involve more of the body in the movement. The important thing is not what movements students make, but that they allow themselves to feel their bodies and muscles responding to the music.

Some children choose to make exaggerated movements, others are more subdued. Whatever they do, encourage them to be aware of their bodies and the energies being released in them through the music. Let them discover that music is not something outside themselves, but that it exists inside them and is able to release energy in them if they let it.

Children may also be invited to sing vowel sounds—"ah," "oh," "oo,' "ee," and the like—to enrich their movement to music. The point of this addition is to show how the sound and movement they create is one with the music and rhythm of the selection being played.

If students are bashful or embarrassed, ask them to close their eyes as they do the exercises. "That way, no one else can see you," you might explain. The important thing is to get past the uptightness, past the mental block, past the embarrassment, and *into* the experience. Embarrassment maintains unnecessary tension, and prevents the experience from carrying the student fully into its dynamic.

Another exercise that children love is rhythmic finger-tapping or drumming with the hands on their upper legs or desk tops. Often their feet will spontaneously join in maintaining the rhythm.

When students are allowed to keep drumming for a minute or two, or longer, they seem to enter totally into the rhythm and become one with it. A look of intensity, smiling, laughter, and feelings of release are all signs in the young drummers that energy is beginning to flow and that the body and mind are feeling a oneness. It seems quite probable that the physical act of drumming a rhythm pattern continuously for five minutes or singing for five minutes stimulates the brain's production of endorphins.

One might think such activity would turn a class into a room of hyperkinetic children. Not so. The rhythm patterns created by the students allows their bodies and minds to be realigned and ready for focused study. Often energies that have been blocked in the body or mind are released. There is a great excitement in a child when he or she feels the free flow of energy from within.*

------

*For some entertaining suggestions about how to use music with students, see Steven Halpern's *Music-Making Manual for Non-Musicians*, in both tape and booklet format (see Sound Helps).

Rhythm and Behavior

One of the serendipitous discoveries made while working with rhythm in schools is that it can bring about major transformations in the behavior of certain students.

When I first began teaching in the California public schools in 1971, I was assigned to a noisy class of junior high students. The rowdiest was a hyperkinetic red-headed lad named Darby. His self-appointed mission was to sabotage my control of the class.

I invited him to the front of the room, sat him behind a conga drum, and had him begin translating his energy into sound by beating the drum with his hands. After drumming loud and hard for about twelve seconds, he stopped.

"I didn't tell you to stop," I said. "Continue playing."

He began, then soon stopped again.

I repeated my "Continue playing" command again and again, for the next five minutes while the class watched with rapt attention.

After five minutes of drumming, something clicked in Darby's consciousness. Perhaps the rhythms had triggered a balancing of his cerebral hemispheres. At any rate, he realized that he was having fun playing music on the conga drum.

He was also exhausted!

When I allowed him to stop drumming and go back to his seat, he was a model of good behavior for the rest of that day.

After class, he came up to me and told me that he had always been interested in music, and he asked if I would become his guitar teacher.

Open to the challenge, I accepted Darby as a private student. Within a short time, his considerable energies had been channelled in a constructive manner, and he became the premier teenage guitarist in the city. That day with the conga drum had been a turning point in his life.

Other teachers noticed the startling improvement in his behavior in their classes. They kept looking in on my class to find out what my secret was.

Rhythm and music are wonderful "secrets" for touching the lives of students.

Music and Enhanced Learning

A lot has been written lately about enhancing the learning environment. Many new techniques have been proposed and, in some cases, implemented.

Music provides one of the most powerful tools to access new dimensions and new capacities of the mind. The process involves using music played in the background as a catalyst during the process of instruction.

Some of the techniques that involve music-listening are Suggestology®, Super Learning®, Accelerated Learning, and Optimalearning®, all of which stem from the innovative discoveries of the Bulgarian psychiatrist and educator, Dr. Georgi Lozanov. Lozanov's accelerated learning techniques utilize music, literature, visual design, theater, and drama in the learning environment. Music is helpful in setting a joyful and relaxed atmosphere that helps produce a revitalizing effect on the individual and stimulate whole-brain activity.

But be forewarned: accelerated learning does not work with just *any* music. The secret is to select music that tends to balance, harmonize, and synchronize the activities of both halves of the brain. Lozanov has found success using the slow (adagio) portions of certain Baroque composers. It is important to recognize that most Baroque music is played rather up-tempo. The faster sections of classical and other genres of music are simply too "interesting" to be suitable.

If you study using some of these "interesting" musical selections, you may not have much success; you'll probably find yourself *paying attention to the music rather than to what you want to be learning.*

Studies in the United States and Europe have found that the "Anti-Frantic"® series of compositions are compatible with this approach to learning. Even though this music does not possess the "orthodox" tempo of 60 beats per minute, it has been shown to facilitate whole-brain functioning.

It is also of more than passing interest to remember that Dr. Lozanov lives in a communist country, and does not have free access to a varied record library. In his experiments, he chose the best of what was available to him. Thus his choices should not be construed as dogma. We have found that several other tempos—or no "beat" at all—can produce a similar effect.*

An Educational Model for the Future

Results indicate that this enriched learning environment may well be an educational model of the future. The theory behind accelerated learning is that a unique combination of music and art acts as a setting for learning and serves as a carrier for large amounts of information to both hemispheres of the brain.

How does music work in learning? At one level, music helps calm the body and mind, enabling the person to be a more effective learner. It is further hypothesized that the special music helps balance, harmonize, and synchronize the brain and allows the body to have its energy flow in harmony with its own rhythms rather than the rhythm of the music.

Results of Lozanov's methods include first-graders who were able, under superlearning conditions, to complete a two-year curriculum in two months. In other studies, adults learned to speak a foreign language fluently in one month.

A recent development that may enhance this superlearning effort is found in my *Soundwave 2000®* series. *The Joy of Learning*, an adagio-style recording specifically composed for fostering learning and studying, includes a subtle, simulated heartbeat to further entrain the listener's mind and body into appropriate breathing and brain-wave patterns.

---

*As of this writing, to my knowledge, mine is the only music beside classical music that has been studied in light of Lozanov's approach to learning and whole-brain functioning.

In addition, *The Joy of Learning* features specific positive programming suggestions interwoven into the music at very low volume levels. In this programming technique, which I call Harmonic Affirmation®, the suggestions are played in harmony with the chordal structure of the music, so that the words become part of the orchestration.

This is one small way in which technology helps us catch up to the needs of education in the 80s. According to educator, author, and philosopher Jean Houston, we are still educating people using learning techniques developed in 1825 for life in the 1980s. It's about time that we started using techniques designed for contemporary people.

Helping Yourself—and Your Children

What can you do for yourself or your children if an accelerated learning course is not available in your area and in your field of interest?

At the very least, you can complement your study time with a background of relaxing music.

According to many letters, students from grade school through college have started substituting relaxing music for the rock music they customarily kept on while they studied.

A typical report: "At first, I missed the big beat, and I didn't like the soft music," wrote one teenage student. "But I *did* like the fact that my grade point average jumped a whole point."

Remember: if you are a parent helping your child study, put on some relaxing background music. If you are a student yourself, try the same.

What music to play?

Experiment. Most people find relaxing music best. Try some of the slow portions of traditional classical music. Try some contemporary compositions. Discover for yourself what kinds of sound or music best create for you a soothing, nondistracting ambience.

Remember, if the music is too interesting or too involving, it may capture your attention away from the learning. If you find yourself consciously listening to the music, it's probably not the right music to foster learning.

Lifelong Learning

Learning doesn't end the day that one receives a diploma. In fact, adult education is another hallmark of the self-help, self-responsible generation we live in.

Time is of the essence. Adults often can't afford to take all the time they would like to learn some new language or skill. Research today is exploring the way the brain works in order to facilitate learning that can be applied in the worlds of business, management, professional sports, and communication.

Sound Education in the Business World

A growing number of companies are beginning to realize that a healthy employee is a productive employee. They understand that the expense of setting up a health club for all of the staff, not only top executives, pays off in lower absentee rates and higher productivity. Fitness programs are now seen not just in the big companies, such as Levi-Strauss, Shaklee, and Lockheed, but in smaller companies as well.

It's all part of a trend away from simply treating illness and toward keeping people well. Many companies offer large preventive health-care packages, including not only physical fitness gyms, but also seminars on stress management, clinics to stop smoking, and counseling on nutrition and diet.

If there could be integrated into the planning of such health-care packages a little know-how and information about the effects of sound and music on health, the general effectiveness of most of those preventive programs could be enhanced.

That's where sound education for adults comes in.

For example, while great care is often taken in choosing the color of an exercise-and-fitness room, little notice is taken of the sources of sound pollution there. Physically, the decibel level could be cut by putting sound-absorbent material on the floors, walls, and ceilings. Psychologically, appropriate music could be added—music that relaxes people and allows bodies to find their own rhythms.

As people become more aware of the relationship between noise level, efficiency, stress, and disease in the office, workers will help to bring about the required changes. Through the appropriate use of sound conditioning, personalized background music delivery systems, and quieter office machines, we look forward to the day when offices are healthier, happier, and more productive environments.

We also look forward to the day that, whenever people talk about education and holistic health, they will include an awareness of music and the sound environment.

Chapter 12

SOUND PRINCIPLES

Composing for Health

Music therapists search the library of classical, sacred, semiclassical, and popular music to find selections that can be used to promote relaxation and psychotherapeutic growth. There are many choices, but they are limited in general to compositions written and performed primarily as works of art.

With our current knowledge of how music can help produce relaxation and other psychodynamic effects, it seems that a new avenue is opening to composers and musicians. They can begin composing and performing with the listener's health in mind.

This alternative genre of music, which began to develop in the 1970s, is currently experiencing a dramatic increase in both compositions and listening audience. Perhaps for the first time in Western civilization, a number of contemporary composers are very consciously creating music to elicit the relaxation response and to facilitate the healing process. Composers such as myself, Iasos, Paul Horn, Kitaro, Georgia Kelly, Joel Andrews, and many others feel and acknowledge a responsibility to their audiences to produce music that is harmonious, uplifting, and pleasing.

Granted, you won't find such music among the Top-40 hits. Yet, how monotonous the sounds of the forest would be if the music came only from the top-ten birds. In 1982, a study of lifestyle values conducted by a prestigious California think-tank, SRI International, stated that 40 million Americans want to be healthier and more relaxed.

Granted, there are levels of quality in this new music, as in any field of music. But the new orientation has made a quantum leap over the orientation prevailing in the traditional, commercial music industry.

The Principle of Beneficial Sounds

Our bodies can discriminate between beneficial and detrimental sounds.

This principle operates under almost all conditions. Even with our ears completely blocked, the body still responsds to sounds. You can be strengthened or weakened by music, whether or not you hear it.

Even when your mind and feelings seem to be delighted and fascinated by certain sounds, such as a familiar song, it is possible that the sound is detrimental to your health.

There may be times when you feel bored by a certain piece of music, but your body is deriving nourishment from the sounds.

At other times, the music playing in the background may be nourishing you in a manner somewhat analogous to intravenous feeding. You are being fed without involving your mind, feelings, or your conscious attention.

The point here is not to focus on the harmful effects of noise, but rather on the wide variety of ways that our bodies and minds can be enormously helped by certain sounds. Our goal is to make people, including composers and performers, aware of this fact.

When you are surrounded by healthy sounds, you can be invigorated, energized, and balanced. The right music can add a great deal to your general health and well-being.

You can get a lot more out of life when you get a lot more into music. Nourishing music may be found among a variety of kinds of music. *The secret is to pay attention to what's happening to you as you listen.*

New Criteria for Evaluating Music

It is important to see what this orientation implies. It is entirely possible that we are witnessing the development of a new principle of aesthetics in Western music.

When we reflect on how and why composers compose as they do, let us consider that the sounds and the culture often affect composers. In the eighteenth century, composers traveled everywhere in horse-drawn carriages. It is not surprising that the rhythms of their music went clip-clop as well.

In the twentieth century, composers travel by car or airplane. It is not surprising to find music full of drones and clusters and other industrial sound effects.

Likewise, the railroads had a powerful influence on the development of jazz rhythm and harmonics. The rhythm of the train pulling over the tracks is reflected in certain drum beats. The wail of the steam whistles of passing trains, a manifestation of a Doppler shift, suggests the slides from major to minor thirds in blues chords. The concern in most cases was to make the music *expressive*, rather than *relaxational*.

Traditionally, questions of evaluation and appreciation about music were made on the basis of theory and technique. Performers were usually judged on their technical virtuosity, and compositions were analytically scrutinized according to their structure and form as well as their ability to satisfy public tastes and fashion in entertainment.

From the *health perspective*, on the other hand, the primary concern over a piece of music is whether or not it helps tune our "human instrument." The question is not, "Does it entertain?" but, "Is it healthful?"

We are less interested in prodigious feats of technical prowess than with how we *feel* when the music is over. It is less, "Does it challenge the analytic intellect?" than, "Does it increase the alpha and theta wave frequences in the brain and enhance the balance and phase coherence between left and right hemispheres?"

And perhaps underlying all these questions, "Was this performance performed with love?"

The Principle of Performance

If you are planning to use a piece of music for your health, pay attention to that particular performance for its ability to produce energy, harmony, and balance in yourself.

Did you ever notice that if you listen to three different recordings of Pachelbel's *Canon in D* you have three different physiological and emotional responses? In each recording the musicians are playing the identical set of notes. What makes the difference?

Is it the tempo? Is it the recording quality? Is it the artwork on the album jacket?

Dr. John Diamond, reporting in his book *Your Body Doesn't Lie*, has scientifically observed groups of people listening to different recordings of the opening of the third movement of Beethoven's *Ninth Symphony*. Although he is able to verify through meter readings that listeners are more energized by a certain performance more than any other, he says that he has learned to observe the same differences easily in a group by watching what he calls the Respiratory Energy Spontaneous Pulse (RESP).

"If I play a performance of Beethoven's *Ninth* conducted by Furtwangler, I will see almost within seconds that the entire group is breathing synchronously, all their chests seem to be moving in unison."

This uniform respiratory pulsation in the group happens only where there is what Diamond terms a "high energy performance." Many other interpretations of this same piece of music do not produce the synchronous breathing response.

In these other cases, the conductor seems to lack what Manfred Clynes in *Sentics: The Touch of Emotions* calls the "inner pulse"; it is a kind of empathy with an internally conducted tempo and time signature felt by the composer of the music.

It is as if the music itself—the composition—has its own true inner pulse. When the conductor and performers are in touch with this inner pulse, the music they create can produce the highest energy in the listeners.

Dr. Diamond claims that with subtle behavioral kinesiology testing, it is possible to tell if a conductor or soloist has the pulse, and even to tell when either may have lost it during the performance.

Music is a carrier wave for consciousness.

Thus, if a musical selection has an inherent potential to energize or balance us, its effect may be lessened or lost by a conductor or performer who is under personal stress, filled with painful or destructive emotions, or out of touch with the composition's inner pulse.

An easy test is simply to take a relaxed posture and watch your breath as you listen. If you are breathing more shallowly and randomly, it is likely that rhythmic attunement is not happening. If you seem to be breathing more deeply and regularly, the performance is probably in resonance with the pulse of your body.

The Principle of Music and Energy

Music and sound may be used as sources of energy and as a way to correct energy imbalances in the body and mind.

This is a sound principle that was treated throughout Part I. Here it will be enough to summarize how music and energy are connected.

We have seen that music seems able to activate basic life-energy, to stir emotional energy, to reduce one's vulnerability to stress, to promote speedier healing, and to balance the activity in the right and left hemispheres of the brain.

Certain music, especially when used with appropriate imagery, can help raise pain thresholds (as with patients in chronic pain or in certain patients in the last and most painful stages of cancer). The music seems to have an effect both as a kind of analgesia as well as an anesthetic.

Psychologically, certain music seems to have a therapeutic effect on our relationships with ourselves, others, and indeed with the whole world. We are not sure how it achieves this transformation, but it seems to energize us to work through and change our negative attitudes.

Psychiatrist John Diamond does not hesitate to underline music's unique therapeutic function. "Used correctly and appropriately reinforced, it is possible with music," he writes, "to achieve in minutes the results of perhaps years of psychotherapy."

This is not to say that all music is therapeutic for all people and for all psychological illnesses. If that were so, we could simply pipe music into all mental institutions tomorrow morning and have all the patients cured by lunch time.

It is important to stress that we are still at the primitive stages of learning the wide range of therapeutic effects music can have. We have clarified some sound principles, but we have miles to go before we master the energies of music and sound. In the larger field of psychotherapy, music remains virtually an untapped resource. We can say, however, that music and sound as healing and energizing forces are potentially available to all of us.

The Principle of Consciousness and Change

Music and sound may be used as tools of consciousness. By becoming conscious of something, we can effect a change in it. Only the business person who is aware of an opportunity to make a profit can take advantage of that opportunity. Only the person who becomes conscious of an inappropriate attitude or behavioral habit can begin to change it.

Growth, change, and improvement happen because somebody becomes aware of the possibility and takes action to bring it about.

A growing consciousness is usually a sign of health. It is also an essential basis for self-help and a guiding element in self-responsibility. For this reason, the tools and procedures that help expand consciousness are very important.

We use the term consciousness here in a generic sense, to refer to any and all parts of the spectrum of awareness—sensing, thinking, feeling, intuiting, knowing, and the like. Further, the content of consciousness is taken to cover the entire sweep of subject matter available to our conscious and unconscious.

For many of the following expressions of this principle, we are indebted to Dr. Helen Bonny. They are reported in her major address to the American Association of Music Therapy in Philadelphia, 1983. Dr. Bonny points out that through music you can relive or reorganize a past event in a similar way at a different level of experience.

It is an axiom of psychotherapy that if a client did not in childhood complete a necessary stage of psychological growth, such as getting beyond dependence upon the mother, the client will tend to recreate a similar dependent relationship with another person, as if to offer the self another chance to complete the missed growth step. Such a new relationship represents not only itself, but symbolically replays the original relationship with the mother. Unless the client comes to consciousness and works through the dependence issue, the pattern of forming dependent relationships will probably continue—that is, after the present relationship is unsuccessful, another dependent one will be formed, and so on.

In a guided imagery and music session, the imagination may create a similar dependent relationship, which in its basic structure reveals, in microcosm, holologically, the entire history—past, present, and future—of the client's relational pattern, usually with its affective components.

The therapist and client can then work therapeutically with the imaginal material. Since this material is usually far less threatening than a real-life situation, the client is more open to insight and consciousness.

Associative Recall

In its deeper layers, our consciousness is filled with myriad images that can provide an unendingly rich source of solutions for problems and a creative base for untold personal psychological wealth.

The musical stimuli often evoke "emotion-producing concomitants" to the imaginal material. Music-generated mood states help the therapist and the therapeutic process by helping bring blocked emotional areas to conscious attention for purposes of catharsis and self-understanding.

Associative recall facilitated by music-listening, points out brain researcher Juan Roederer in discussing music and brain functioning, is less a photographic imaging of the original scene than a hologram-like representation of it. In his masterful article "Music Perceptions and Basic Functions of the Human Brain," written for

Manfred Clyne's collection *Music, Mind and Brain* (1982), he describes how "information of the object stimulus is mapped onto the whole domain of the image."

He shows how, in associative recall, an enactment of the original event can be cued by a very small segment of it. Thus playing the first four notes of Beethoven's *Fifth Symphony* can trigger replay of the entire symphony within the mind of a knowledgeable listener. In therapy with music, bits and pieces of imagery and affect, like those first four notes of Beethoven's *Fifth Symphony*, can trigger, for example, a replay of the client's entire dependence relationship pattern.

Under proper conditions, music-listening becomes a versatile tool for exploring unusual levels of consciousness: it allows entrance into metaphoric modes of experience; it may be used to facilitate changes of level of consciousness within a field of non-ordinary states of consciousness; and through its auditory stimuli it may activate the imagination and interweave visual, kinesthetic, and other auditory responses in that faculty.

The Sound Principle of Individuality

In a sound diet, individual needs and tastes must be taken into consideration.

The bottom line in listening to music for health is your own "response-ability." It is your responsibility to tune into your own tastes, your own moods, and your current place in your own biological cycle.

Just what music will work best for you?

We can't tell you. Only you can discover that for yourself.

As a point of departure, try some of the suggestions that we offer in the last section of this book. Don't be surprised if music that works well for someone else may not work well for you, or vice versa. One person's music may be another person's noise.

Experiment.

And enjoy! In the final analysis—at least at this stage of research—you must be the judge.

Chapter 13

SOUND CONDITIONING

Dimensions of Conditioning

Conditioning is a behavioral learning process first clarified early in the twentieth century by the Russian physiologist Ivan B. Pavlov. Most everyone has heard of Pavlov's dog, who was trained to salivate at the sound of a bell.

Once rewards (or "reinforcements," as the learning psychologists call them) and punishment are added to the conditioning process, it takes on new dimensions. Conditioning becomes a paradigm for learning and education. Rewards in the form of good grades and approval motivate many a young student to excel in school.

Conditioning can work on conscious and unconscious levels. Even subtle rewards or reinforcement, such as suggestions from someone we respect, can promote the conditioning process.

We are very open to suggestion at every level of our being. Most of us are familiar with verbal suggestions that affect our conscious behavior, such as getting us to read a certain book, see a certain film, go to a certain restaurant, buy a certain kind of car. But suggestions can also affect us at deeper levels.

As documented in his book, *Getting Healthy Again*, Dr. O. Carl Simonton's treatments of terminal cancer patients include listening to a cassette program in which Dr. Simonton suggests that the patient's healthy cells can attack and destroy the cancerous ones. And the suggestions seem to work. Simonton's approach is based on the theory that every cell in the body is able to respond to mental suggestions.

Beyond Mere Relaxation

Conditioning goes beyond the relaxation response; it taps into a person's self-regulating mechanisms. In certain research and clinical practice, including that of Dr. O. Carl Simonton in cancer research, reported in *Getting Healthy Again*, music is being used as a catalyst or carrier to facilitate mental suggestion.

As we have already seen, certain musical selections bring with them an imagery-laden content of their own. Certain other selections do not. These "neutral" compositions, which may be found among the music of both classical and New Age composers, seem to allow the body and mind to move into a brain-wave pattern in which the listeners seem able to visualize their personal therapeutic imagery and utilize their own mental self-healing capacities.

Appropriate music can also help get the person into the frame of mind that will facilitate the healing treatment of another modality. As Simonton has shown, sound and music often prove to be a valuable adjunct and complement to standard medical practice.

The right kind of music can activate right-hemisphere functioning and release a flow of imagery, even with those who cannot normally visualize very well either on their own or in response to someone else's spoken command. With practice—and the right music—almost anyone can develop imaginative abilities.

One of the challenges in using music as an adjunct to other healing modalities is to *choose the correct music*. In choosing music for patients to visualize their healthy cells attacking the cancer cells, some people may find martial music helpful, others favor more reflective music. It does not seem that any one selection or any one type of music works best for all people in all situations.

What does seem true is that music can be helpful in the treatment of many health problems. Simonton is using music to intensify mental suggestion in cancer treatment. Others are using music and suggestion in helping patients develop self-regulating health protection for cardiovascular disease, epilepsy, and other catastrophic illnesses.

Certain autonomous and unconscious self-regulating physical

systems—such as the heart, the digestive process, the endorphin-circulating peptide system, the immune system, and the autonomic nervous system—were always believed to be out of conscious control (and therefore able to be treated only with drugs and other chemical substances). These systems are now known to be affected by mental suggestion and creative imagery.

Clinical research is showing that mental suggestion and/or self-conditioning may be used not only to help heal diseased parts, but to maintain and intensify healthy ones.

The unspoken assumption is that healing and growth is accomplished with energy, and that energy is being released through conditioning. What clinical research is demonstrating about the human self-regulating system is the ancient adage that *energy follows thought*. If the desired result is thought of, imaged, or affirmed, energy seems to be attracted to the healing process and the result is accomplished sooner. Music is being used to facilitate such thoughts, images, and affirmations.

Music is also being used in self-conditioning focused on correcting unhealthy unconscious thought patterns. Some unconscious thought patterns that can control people's lives include, "I'm fat because it runs in our family," or "I'm poor and I'll probably always be poor."

If you think that you are fat and keep conditioning yourself with unconscious thought patterns to reinforce that idea, then you are probably generating energy to keep yourself fat. This often includes food addictions that will keep you overweight. If you believe that you are poor and destined to be so, your thought energy can help create conditions to fulfill that prophecy.

Your thoughts can work for you or against you. The choice is yours.

Reprogramming Unconscious Patterns

If you have identified in yourself some areas that you would like to work on—such as achieving an ideal weight or becoming a more effective learner—it is possible to reprogram your patterns in a more constructive way. If you haven't, you might gain some insights and ideas for improving your health by consulting with any one of many health professionals who offer such help, either in workshops, groups, or individual contexts.

The important thing is to get in touch with what you want to work on. Once you know the result you want, the following information may be helpful to you.

The process moves along easier and faster if you program your unconscious patterns while in an altered state of consciousness using methods such as deep relaxation, hypnosis or self-hypnosis, or deep relaxation—all of which may be intensified using appropriate music as a catalyst.

Reprogramming usually takes time and patient repetition. Patterns established in childhood and acted out for decades are not easily unseated from their positions of power over our lives.

One of the most effective psychotechnologies involves the use of cassettes rather than working with a therapist in a one-on-one situation.

However, not everyone is psychologically able to handle self-reprogramming. Such self-care is not for everybody. If you have any questions or doubts, contact professional guidance before attempting this technique.

Taped programs are not a substitute for medical care. If you experience seizures of any kind, or if you have any other neurological or neurorespiratory disease, consult your physician for suggestions concerning use of such tapes. If you suffer from any emotional or mental disorder, or are already undergoing psychotherapy, consult your psychotherapist or physician about using such tapes.

But for those who are able to use them, the advantages of tapes are many. They are much less expensive than a therapist. They are convenient and don't require that you go to an office. Cassettes are available for playing at any time of day or night, and some may even be used while sleeping. Tapes won't get bored repeating the same message to you over and over. Finally, such a wide range of taped suggestion programs are currently available that the cassette you may need is probably already on the market.

According to feedback from tape users, tapes often seem to be at least as effective for their purpose as working with another human being. Moreover, many people already working with a therapist find listening to cassettes a supportive adjunct to therapy.

Music in Reprogramming Unconscious Patterns

Tapes to help in reprogramming unwanted unconscious patterns are often enhanced by music that helps put the listener into a state of relaxation and balance. In this more receptive state, all parts of the brain are receptive. *The music acts as a carrier wave, bringing the reprogramming message directly into the mind's deeper, unconscious levels*, where the new pattern will ultimately reside.

There are an ever-growing number of organizations offering cassette tapes for reprogramming. Many of these are commercially available. Many are easily accessible via mail order. A self-help tape typically has the desired affirmations and suggestions in an environment of balanced and harmonic music, white noise or nature sounds. Sometimes the words are clearly audible; at other times they may be inaudible.

Creating Your Own Images

Some people may wish to create their own tapes for their own specific needs. The following comments may be helpful.

Some musical selections work better than others on self-help tapes. When making your own tapes, choose the music that works best for you. If you are incorporating verbal suggestions, you will need to establish an appropriate balance between the volume of the words and the volume of the music. Professional producers of such tapes sometimes spend as much time on this detail as they do on recording the spoken suggestions.

There is much more to making a subliminal tape than merely speaking the words at a lower volume. Some tapes on the market use sophisticated computerized techniques to encode the words into the chords and melodies of the music.

But, whatever the process, the principle is clear: *The unconscious mind can hear, perceive, absorb, and act upon these suggestions, even if the conscious mind cannot hear them.*

When such subliminal conditioning is done to you without your knowledge and consent, it is an infringement upon you at many levels. *But when you consciously choose to use current knowledge about subliminal conditioning to enhance your life, then you are taking a positive step towards actualizing your full potential.*

One final note. Copyright laws allow you to create a tape program containing prerecorded and copyrighted music *for your own personal use.* It is illegal, however, for you to make copies of your self-help material that contains such music for sale to others. Such a sale is an infringement of the copyright law.

If you think that your material is very succesful and you want to make it public, licensing agreements for use of the music on your tape may be arranged, in many cases, with the recording artist or publisher of the music.

The field of sound conditioning promises to be a powerful tool in helping people live more fully. Using psychologically effective music as an environment for conditioning is growing in popularity. Much research is needed in order to discover how the process may be made more effective and efficient.

Sound Addiction

Is it possible to become addicted to sounds that are really unhealthy for us?

It certainly is. We can become addicted to certain sounds and rhythms just as we can become addicted to alcohol, caffeine, chocolate, nicotine, or gambling.

People who are addicted to a substance discover that they can't go very long without it. They need their fix.

It is likely that many young people are addicted to rock music. When they go for very long without it, they seem to begin manifesting withdrawal symptoms.

Directors of fitness centers say that customers complain when the usual loud rock or disco music is not playing during workout times.

Dr. John Diamond, who has tested the capacity of musical selections to weaken or strengthen muscles, says that most people's muscles weaken when rock music with a stopped-anapestic beat is playing.

As we mentioned in an earlier chapter, the stopped-anapestic rhythm is the name given to one of the standard rock rhythm patterns. This beat—short, short, long, pause—was first popularized in the 1960s. Today it is heard in much of pop and rock music.

This rhythm is unhealthy because it opposes the natural beat of the heart and is contrary to the rhythm of the arterial pulsations. Very simply, the external stimulus of the drummer overpowers the internal rhythm of the body. It confuses the heart and body, thus weakening them.

Switching

According to Dr. Diamond, when the weakening beat is listened to, a phenomenon called "switching" occurs. That is, symmetrical functioning between the two cerebral hemispheres is lost.

This loss creates a number of problems. Switching introduces subtle perceptual difficulties and many other manifestations of stress, such as decreased performance, hyperactivity, restlessness, increased errors, general inefficiency, and reduced decision-making capacity.

Nevertheless, repeated exposure to this apparently addictive specific rock beat causes people to seek it out. It becomes the beat of choice. It is missed when it is not present.

According to Dr. Diamond, "It is as if the switching introduced by the rock beat has become the normal rather than the abnormal physiological state."

Once switching becomes ingrained through constant listening and frequent dancing, a serious problem is introduced. If an average subject listens to the stop anapestic beat, all indicator muscles will test weaker than normal. However, if the subject has been switched, the opposite will often occur: he or she will test *strong* to the anapestic beat and *weak* to healthful music.

In Diamond's words (his italics): *"It is as if his body no longer can distinguish what is beneficial and what is harmful. In fact, his body now actually chooses that which is destructive over that which is therapeutic."*

Turning down the volume does not affect switching. The phenomenon occurs even at low levels. This is a tell-tale sign of the way sound addiction operates.

Noise, in contrast, is not addictive. Although muscles will test weak when the noise level rises above 80 dBA, explains Diamond, as soon as the noise level subsides the indicator muscle will test strong again.

Getting Unswitched

Is it possible to get unswitched?

Yes, there are at least two ways.

One of the most ancient and effective ways is to spend some time outdoors. Get in communion with the sounds and smells of nature—in the forest, by a stream, at the seashore. We are living biosystems, like all life-forms on earth, and we are electromagnetically tuned to the resonant frequencies of our planet.

Virtually all ancient religions encouraged communion with nature and attunement to the earth. This is now being understood in terms of contemporary physics; it relates to the entrainment of our bodies with the electromagnetic energy fields of the earth itself. Tuning into nature and the energies of the earth is one effective way of getting unswitched.

Another way is by changing your sound diet to music that evokes responses of symmetry from both hemispheres of the brain. Available for this is a wide variety of classical and New Age music. From a "sound health" perspective, good music is therapeutic. (A note of caution: Even good music will likely weaken muscles and thus prove anti-therapeutic when played at volume levels where sound distortion occurs.)

In ancient times, the original orientation of music was magical, ceremonial, and therapeutic. It is interesting that we are witnessing a "return to roots" in the midst of the culture of the computer.

The questions that underlie all this research is: What is good music? How does one find appropriate music for one's specific needs? How can one know what is therapeutic, life-supporting, uplifting or healthful?

Music Composed to Assist Healing

The state of the movement for sonic sanity and sound health is at about the same stage that the health food movement and the no-smoking movements were a decade ago.

In the early 1970s, much of the food on supermarket shelves was processed, artificially colored, artificially flavored, and laced with preservatives. Today, in contrast, major food chain stores include sections for health foods and vitamins. We see alfalfa sprouts and tofu in the produce section, yogurt in the dairy case, herbal teas beside the caffeinated ones, unprocessed vegetable oils on the shelf for salad and baking needs, soups and other packaged items without preservatives. Many major brands herald the fact that their soft drinks contain no sugar, no caffeine, no preservatives, and no artificial coloring.

This marks a major shift in consciousness of the consumer toward health. It also marks a change in the mentality of food manufacturers. At least they are now willing to include healthful items alongside processed junk food.

Up until now, much of what has been available in the marketplace and the airwaves relates to sonic junk food—the processed, artificial sounds of canned music or the slick, overproduced sounds of many popular recordings. In their own way, much of punk rock, heavy metal, and the new wave movement represent a protest against the artificiality of much of the contemporary music industry.

The analogy between food and sound continues when we realize that, in both cases, manufacturers are much more clearly oriented toward making products designed to make a profit than they are to making products designed to enhance the health of the consumer.

Just as a decade ago virtually no major food producers outside of the health food industry were interested in producing "health" foods for people concerned about their health, so today virtually no major music producers are interested in producing music for people concerned about their health.

Indeed, very few composers and performers create music in order to facilitate and enhance the health of their listeners. Certainly, very few musicians are trained in the therapeutic aspects of composition and performance. Probably most aren't interested in it. But there are more and more who are growing interested.

The new genre of music produced by such musicians is variously called new age music, anti-frantic music, alternative music, space music, mellow music, or world music. Its primary intent is to uplift the body, mind, and spirit of the listener.

Healthful Music

With so much destructive sound and noise assaulting us on the one hand, and so much potential for using music in healthy ways available to us on the other, what is a person to do?

Years ago, I learned that it was possible to complement a scientific approach to this question by asking my body instead of my brain, "What kind of music would you like? What music will help tune you and heal you?" . . . and listening for its answer.

In 1969, frustrated with what I found in the existing literature, and needing something legal, nonaddictive, and inexpensive, I set out to create a new kind of music. I knew, in my heart of hearts, that I had no choice but to dedicate my life to researching and composing music for health and healing. In early 1975, after six years of laboratory, clinical, and anecdotal research, I published my first recording.

While many listeners welcomed my new healthful music as a "refreshing wind on the music scene," others treated it with a mixture of disbelief, derision, and apathy. Neither the media nor the music industry were interested in music related to health. "Where was the big beat?" "Where was the hit single?" "Where was the hook?"

The president of Columbia Records' Special Products Division, plus several other heads of major recording labels, liked the music and recognized its value, but frankly told me, "It has no commercial potential." They advised me to produce and market the record by myself. "Establish a track record of sales," they told me, "before you approach us again. See if people will buy this music."

When I started out, the only outlets I could convince to carry my records, which were the only ones of their kind in those early days, were health food stores or bookstores. I also made them available at concerts and by direct mail. The rest, as they say, is history.

Spurred on by my success as a pioneer and role model, a number of other independent artists have produced and released their own recordings of gentle and uplifting music.

Major record stores and other chains are now beginning to stock a representative sampling of this new music. And they are pleasantly surprised at their sales success.

A simple way of distinguishing the difference in orientation between the new music and pop music is to look at titles. On the Top-40 list we see "Love to Love You, Baby," "Let's Get It On," "I Want to Do Something Freaky to You," or "Love Hurts." In New Age music we see titles such as "Invocation," "Invitation," "Elixir," "Eventide," "Dawn," "Bird of Paradise," and "Mother of Pearl."

The Structure of Music

Most traditional music selections are based on cycles of tension and release.

Psychologically, the structural form of such compositions is designed to create a sense of anticipation followed by a sense of relief. Structurally, they achieve their primary emotional effect through conditioning. *They create tension and sustain it*. As long as the listener's mind keeps anticipating the final resolution of the music, the listener is not truly at rest.

This "anticipation response" is at the foundation of almost all musical structures used in most classical and popular music. Such music does not seem to work well with the natural relaxation response mechanisms already built into the healthy person's body and mind.

While such tension-release music may prove interesting to the analytic mind, exciting to the emotions, or helpful in generating dramatic imagery that the music therapist may use in psychotherapy, it is not structurally designed to decompress and de-stress us.

We are not putting down forms of music that do not fit the criteria for facilitating the relaxation response. Far from it. We recommend listening to and enjoying a wide variety of music—classical, folk, popular, jazz, and so forth. But listen *only* to what you want, when you want, and how loud you want.

When, however, you want to relax deeply and be refreshed or bathed by the sound, you will need to use appropriate music. Selections that tend to build up emotional tension, stir excitement, or make you want to sing and dance probably won't fill the bill.

A New Musical Form

There is more to the world of music than can be found in the ethnocentrically biased music of Western Europe of the past few centuries. Unfortunately, we have been so culturally conditioned to compose and respond to music in fixed ways that we often tend to forget that there are many other ways of composing and responding to music.

Throughout history, certain composers have sought to expand the range of what constitutes "music." Typically, their attempts were misunderstood in the beginning. Only with the passing of time and the perspective of history have we come to accept the works of revolutionary composers such as Beethoven and Stravinsky, whose new musical forms were not understood by the critics of their own day.

In typical fashion, critics in the media and in academia have tended not to understand the forms of New Age music. Happily, many scientists, medical people, and many thousands of listeners do understand. They understand that some modern composers are more interested in "orchestrating human instruments" than in composing for the instruments of the standard orchestra or to show off prodigious displays of digital dexterity.

Many of my own music compositions do not rely on the traditional building blocks of Western music. In the "Anti-Frantic Alternative"® series, for example, you won't find a melody that you can hum, a snappy rhythm, or a recognizable harmonic progression. Indeed, it is for precisely these reasons that it works as well as it does.

If the music had all the usual cues of predictability and tonality that most music has, it would fall into the same trap of triggering your emotions and manipulating your breathing and heartbeat.

My personal goal as a composer has always been to serve, to uplift, and to harmonize others through music. The goal of this music is to allow the body and mind of the listener to choose whatever response mode that it wants and needs to operate at a higher level of efficiency.

Although this music is not what people usually call "classical music," historical precedent might be found in the chamber music of the royal courts of eighteenth- and nineteenth-century Europe, or in the ceremonial and meditational court music of ancient China and Egypt.

Perhaps it is the classical music of the New Age. Although much is improvised, it's not really jazz. It also contrasts sharply with the typical canned music found in elevators or department stores. Again and again, people report that this music helps bring more peace and harmony into a home or business environment than commercially popular music. In fact, in unpublished experiments conducted playing this music in hectic offices and doctors' waiting rooms, it was found that the number of complaints and irritation level in the room lowered perceptibly in minutes.

Marvelous, isn't it? The same acoustical mechanics that allows noise pollution to knock us out of tune with ourselves can be utilized to help keep us in tune with our biological birthright: sound health.

Sonic Sanity

As you learn to pay more attention to how your "human instrument" responds to various pieces of music, you can begin to recognize when music is in harmony with the life-supporting sounds that you need at that time.

More and more authorities, like Dr. Herbert Benson of Harvard Medical School, encourage us to bring more relaxation into our lives. They point out the need for us to create for ourselves an oasis of peace and harmony in the midst of the hectic pace of contemporary life.

By conditioning yourself with some sound nutrition—the vitamins of the air waves—you may not only add years to your life, but life to your years!

In summary, listening to beautiful music is one of the simplest relaxational techniques available. However, since most music was not composed specifically for relaxation, it is not surprising to find that much of it may not fulfill our needs in this regard. What is required is a music that takes into account "human harmonics"—a music that works, biologically and psychologically, with the inner codings of the human instrument.

PART THREE

Sound Spirit

Chapter 14

SOUND WHOLENESS

Music and Wholeness

"My purpose is to create music for all people," wrote classical composer Alan Hovhaness, "music which is beautiful and healing, to attempt what old Chinese painters called 'spirit resonance' in melody and sound."

In this section, we explore the effect that sound and music can have on the human soul, or spirit.

To experience music fully is a holistic experience. It is in essence healthy, vital, therapeutic, and sacred. Thus holistic sound health pertains not only to a sound mind in a sound body, but also to a sound spirit.

It is interesting to note that the old Anglo-Saxon word *hāl* is the origin of four contemporary English words: *hale*, or (healthy), *heal*, *whole*, and *holy*. Music is meant to be an experience that evokes all four meanings. It is not surprising, then, that for many people music is not only a healing force but also a call to holiness and wholeness.

A Principal Source of Healing

What will be the future for natural ways of healing? And how will music be involved?

For one thing, a greater number of people will begin to recognize that music is meant to be more than background, entertainment, or a way to pass the time. They will recognize that music can be a vital link in their own holistic health program.

"The time is fast approaching," wrote Corrine Heline in *Esoteric Music*, (1969), "when people will select their music with the same intelligent care and knowledge they now use to select their food. When that time comes, music will become a principal source of healing for many individuals and social ills, and human evolution will be tremendously accelerated."

To start the day off on a good note, we might learn to take a "sound bath" along with a morning shower. A general musical tune-up and balancing for the body, mind, and spirit might be a fine daily first step. Similarly, when we come home from work, or before we go to bed, we can learn to use music to balance our energies and keep them in harmony.

As we come to learn more and more how vibratory frequencies affect not only bodily vitality and emotional moods, but also spiritual energies, we will learn to compose specific healing symphonies for people to strengthen their diminished or altered vibratory rates and bring them back to their natural state. They will be able to find a way back to their proper pattern of wholeness through the harmonies of music.

One step in that direction will be to have sound-and-color healing rooms in hospitals as well as homes. We might even have healing music stations on radio and television, making the healing properties of music and color available to everyone. Imagine the effect of a radio station broadcasting just five minutes of this music during rush hour. It would truly be a public service.

The energies in music capable of being released for human healing and wholeness are as yet scarcely suspected by the musician and composer, far less by the average person.

The great composer Frederick Delius had a sense of the possibilities when he referred to music as "a revelation, a thing to be reverenced." He went on to say that, "Performances of a great musical work are for us what the rites and festivals of religion were to the ancients—an invitation into the mysteries of the human soul."

A Music Notebook

In his book *The Healing Energies of Music*, Hal A. Lingerman, minister and counselor, recommends keeping a musical notebook in which you recall and make note of the many ways that music has enriched your life physically, emotionally, spiritually. He suggests that you also include some of your most intimate memories associated with music.

As you compile a music notebook, you begin to realize how sound plays an important part in daily life. You can recognize firsthand its potential as a healing environment.

Toward a Science of Sound Health

At present, we have a limited number of scientific ways to test the *therapeutic* efficacy of music in the treatment of different emotional, physical, or spiritual disorders. We have even fewer ways to test the *preventive* efficacy of music, that is, how music can help keep people in sound health.

Clearly, the time is at hand for researchers interested in sound's potential for healing and health to explore and experiment.

One confusing element is that nutrients—whether their source is sound, light, color, vitamin, mineral, or other chemical—seem to work as a team. It is difficult to isolate the effects of one specific healing modality, such as sound, since it is difficult scientifically to exclude other modalities that might influence the effects.

Moreover, music itself has many dimensions—melody, rhythm, harmony, tempo, timbre, volume—which complicates any research. Should we test entire musical selections or only a portion of them? Is it possible that one movement of a symphony has healing properties, but another doesn't?

Again, when we begin to talk about holistic healing, we acknowledge that the body affects the mind, and vice versa, and that the human spirit affects and is affected by both body and mind. This integral funtioning of the whole person is another complexity that precludes creating simple scientific tests to find the effects of music on illness or health.

Intuitively, of course, we know that each time we listen to beautiful music—or create and perform some ourselves—it brings healing and renewal. So, while the researchers explore the precise effects of music on healing and wholeness, there is nothing to stop us from enjoying this wonderful gift.

Finding Your Wholeness Music

At this stage of research, it is up to individuals to find the music to which their bodies, minds, and spirits are most responsive.

Many people already know some of the selections to which they respond. We know of one woman who played Beethoven's *Ode to Joy* daily throughout her pregnancy—even in the delivery room. We know of a depressed man who daily used Handel's *Hallelujah Chorus* to keep his feelings of insecurity from overwhelming him. These people found music that worked for them. For those who have no idea where to turn, we have made some general suggestions in the last section of this book.

If you are looking for specific suggestions, we recommend the discography in the appendix of *Music and Your Mind* by Helen L. Bonny and Louis M. Savary. Hal A. Lingerman's *The Healing Energies of Music* contains literally hundreds of concrete suggestions of music that works for him. They include classical, operatic, folk, spiritual, popular, country, jazz, electronic—for specific moods, temperaments, and situations.

Linderman offers lists of pieces for healing the physical body, relaxing it, energizing it, moving it, becoming aware of its beauty. He offers similar lists for the mind and the spirit. For example, he suggests selections for dealing with anger, depression, fear, boredom, hyperactivity; selections to foster courage and strength, relaxation and reverie, love and devotion, clear thinking and mental power.

We also recommend the catalog listings of Halpern Sounds, Vital Body Distribution Company, Narada, et al. The musical recommendations given in these books and catalogs have been found helpful by a number of people. Most are, however, in no way "medically proven" to be effective in any rigorous scientific sense.

The musical selections suggested by Bonny, Savary, Halpern, and Lingerman—or in the final section of this book—are merely helpful clues to aid your search for the music that will help make you a more whole person.

As you audition certain selections, keep in mind that the particular version makes a great difference relative to the effect of the composition. The stylistic "interpretation" as well as the life-energy and attitude of the performer are of critical importance in influencing the healing capacity of a recording.

Music and Anger

Choosing music to help deal with anger is a good example to discuss. Almost everyone at one time or another finds it important to be able to deal with anger. Yet anger is not a simple phenomenon, nor is the way we deal with it.

"Interestingly," writes Lingerman, "I have found that in times of anger different persons react very differently. Some will go to any extremes to avoid controversy and conflict; others just want to be quiet; still others attack and even look for ways to blow off steam in assertive, fiery, combustible outbursts."

Depending on your temperament and style of dealing with anger, you will find certain selections helpful for airing out anger. Choose pieces that are themselves powerful and large enough to receive, absorb, and contain your angry feelings. Examples include Beethoven's *Egmont Overture*, the last movement of Tchaikovsky's *Fifth Symphony*, Brahms' *Piano Concerto No. 1*, or most any work by Scriabin.

On the other hand, if you are looking for music that might calm your anger and rebalance your emotions, or perhaps even transmute your energy into more constructive activity, Lingerman recommends you listen to Handel's *Harp Concerto*, Schubert's *Prelude to Rosamunde*, or Steven Halpern's and Georgia Kelly's *Ancient Echoes*.

It is important to notice in either approach is that the music—when properly listened to and received—is a holistic experience. It not only offers a means to discharge strong, unwanted feelings, but at the same time it fills your body, mind, and spirit with its own cleansing, healing, and energizing currents.

Certain performers, Artur Rubinstein for example, are aware that they are agents of energy helping others, in Lingerman's words, "To transmute negative feelings into positive emotional outpouring through the medium of music." In an interview, pianist Vladimir Horowitz said that he wanted his playing to bathe the listeners in their whole being—body, mind, emotions, and spirit.

Preparing the Spirit to Listen

But all this great music can have its fullest effect only when you are properly prepared to fully experience it. The more totally you can give yourelf to the music you are experiencing, the more its energies can affect your being. Great music is powerful, but its ability to affect you and revitalize you is lessened if you are tense, resistant, critical, analytic, distracted, impatient, ungrateful, unwilling, or have a closed mind. On the contrary, if you can bring a relaxed body, an open mind, and reverent spirit to the music, it is likely to enter you and renew you.

Again and again, relaxed and open listeners report the sense that the music is playing *through* them, not just around them.

"When I relax enough, it's as though my body is a responsive, vibrating vessel," explained one listener. "I am as responsive and open to the flow of the music's vibrations as to the air around me. The music doesn't get stopped when it gets to me, it flows right through. I don't hinder its passing. But as it passes, it leaves its mark, its energy. Afterwards, I feel differently, more whole, more connected with the world."

See Chapter 17 on Sound Meditation for more specific suggestions for preparing the body, mind, and spirit for listening to great music with a desire for healing and wholeness.

The Performer of Music

While much emphasis has been placed on the listener, there is also an important spiritual and holistic effect on the performer. Music has performing participants (the ones who create the sounds) as well as receptive participants (the ones who listen to the sounds).

The performer needs to tap into the healing energies of the music in order to play it in a way that promotes healing and wholeness. To do this, the performer becomes creatively open. Some prepare meditatively for their performance, connecting themselves to the healing energies of the universe. Others prepare by reciting affirmations about the performance and the effects it will have. Such performers might say, "In this music I am expressing my true self in God's love" or "Each note that I play is a note of love and healing" or "This music carries universal love."

Others focus on the audience and, in meditation beforehand, see the audience as a group of friends who want healing and wholeness. This may be particularly helpful when performing for a room full of critics, who are there to analyze and judge the performance. Some performers also verbally tell their audiences the way that they feel about the music to be performed.

There is little doubt that one's performace will produce more love and healing if the performer can do it out of a loving consciousness, rather than an uptight, nervous, or critical consciousness.

A Performer's Consciousness

There is no question that a performer's feelings and consciousness can be transmitted to the audience in a live concert or recital. One's fear—or love—can be communicated through the music without saying a word. A performer's feelings are somehow also transmitted in the phonograph record.

Certainly, an audience can sense this communication in a live performance. At a recital, if you've ever felt a knot in your stomach

even before the first note was played, you were probably responding
the performer's own anxiety and stomach knot. On the other hand,
a performance can be totally uplifting and enjoyable (even if you
heard some "wrong notes") if the musician was loving what he or
she was playing.

Inner Suggestions

Performers often ask how they can relax enough to put aside the
tension that comes from fear of knowing that their performance is
being judged.

Giving themselves positive suggestions has proved helpful to
many performers.

Russian scientists have shown how such suggestion techniques
can work with artists in many fields. In one series of experiments
with painters, students were trained to relax and, in their imagination, ask a master teacher to assist them as they painted. It was
discovered that untrained art students can being to paint like Rembrandt when they tell themselves in a deeply relaxed state that they
are being helped by Rembrandt, or that Rembrandt is inside them
painting through them.

Dr. Jean Houston and others have been exploring these same
techniques to release the inhibitions and fears of musicians. In her
book *The Possible Human*, she suggests that composers and performers ask for help of a certain master of music whom they ad-
mire or want to learn from.

You can ask for help in an open-ended manner, without limiting
the ways that the help may come. There have been times when you
may feel as if your fingers are actually being moved by someone
else. At other times, you might sense a changed atmosphere or
presence around you. At other times, you may actually hear the
music in your head.

How do you know if it's a master teacher—or just your
superconscious?

Does it matter? It is more important to ask: Is the music that
results of a higher quality?

An Imaginary Film

Workshop leader Tim Gallwey offers musicians a creatively imaginative way of improving performance and liberating healing energies in the music. He suggests this scenario:

You, the performer, consider yourself to be merely playing an actor's part in a film. The true soundtrack has already been recorded and is being dubbed into the film. All you have to do is to express the spirit of this professional soundtrack. Of course, you will be playing all the notes as you do this, knowing you do not have to play them all perfectly since the professional soundtrack will be substituted in the final print of the film.

Performers find that they are able to be much more dynamic and expressive when they belive that what they play will not really be used in the movie (i.e., that is not a "performance").

Researchers have found that this technique improves quality of performance significantly and rapidly, allowing the performer's body, mind, emotions, and spirit to be fully involved and expressed in the musical selection.

Gallwey's way of explaining how this works is to point out that we often act as if we had two selves.

Self One is the analytic and critical self. It tells us what we ought be doing, how the music ought to sound, where our fingers ought to be, and so on. Self One operates mainly from the brain's left hemisphere. It is not wrong, but merely very limited. Most professional musicians have been trained to listen to and play music from Self One.

In the movie technique, we keep Self One busy by putting its attention somewhere else, while we cooperate with what Gallwey calls Self Two, the part of us that listens to, feels and enters into the sound of the music. Self Two allows us to be dynamically and expressively involved in the performance. Self Two is more holistic, for it engages not only the left brain, but the right brain and lower brain as well, generating a response that is physical, mental, and emotional.

Playing from the Center

A fully holistic response would be to involve the spirit and soul in the performance. This is a step beyond Self One and Self Two. It involves playing (or listening) from the center of one's being, which Zen Buddhists call the *hara*.

To be a balanced and centered musician means to play from a balanced and centered posture. One's center is normally thought to be located in the abdominal area slightly below the navel.

A musician can learn to *play from that center*, that is, to play as if the center were the source of the music.

I vividly remember receiving a lesson from a master teacher in which I learned to play from my center. I was actually able to control the ease with which the piano keys could be depressed, by focusing energy directly from my center—as well as by drawing energy from the piano through my fingers into my center. It was a startling experience. That lesson opened up for a me a whole new level of playing music—and playing myself!

Part of the "hear and now" of my training was learning to be totally in the moment, whether playing or listening, rather than worrying about the past notes or future ones. I learned to play without judging, without predicting, without self-doubt.

For must musicians, such openness can be achieved through desire and practice. It can be a most liberating and exhilarating experience.

A Special Something

The spiritual quality of a performance is something beyond professional technique. It is that highly prized extra something that separates the great from the good. It is the quality that brings alive what would otherwise be only a technically perfect surface rendering.

Many great artists don't mind hitting "wrong notes" now and then, for they realize that their performance has that indescribable spiritual quality. They are co-creating with the music, and that is the primary value for them.

A woman who owns a beautiful Steinway baby grand piano but never plays it any more says that she can't bear to hear herself play after attending an Artur Rubenstein concert. How distorted to think that it might be the intention of those who play with great spiritual energy to intimidate the rest of us into silence. Much more likely, the masters would like to inspire us to greater enjoyment and spiritual depth in our own playing.

There is none of us without soul waiting to be expressed.

Enhanced Capabilites

Many musicians have experienced a performance that sounds great and it seems to happen "all by itself." We might be playing a phrase we played many times before, but this time, by some happy accident, it sounds and feels better than we're used to.

When you find yourself suddenly functioning with enhanced capabilities, observe how you feel and how your body is postured. (This is natural biofeedback.) You may learn something that can enhance all your future playing, moving you to a higher level of performance.

You may feel this capacity with just one note. Do not be afraid to focus your musical experience upon a single sound, whether singing or playing an instrument.

Allow the single sound to flow into your consciousness effortlessly. There is no need to strive or to force the sound. Here it within. Let the sound originate deep within the center of your being. Let more and more consciousness and sensitivity awaken within you and fill the tone.

For some, just such a moment as this—playing or singing a single note with the totality of their being—will mark a step in the realization of their spiritual potential.

Chapter 15

SOUND SOUL AND SPIRIT

Expressions of the Soul

Psyche is the Greek word for soul. There are two primary expressions of the human soul that are clearly manifested through sound vibrations in the human body. These two very ordinary and usually very healing human sounds are *crying* and *laughter*.

We all have heard the phrase "a good healthy cry." Allowing tears to flow from the eyes, allowing the body to shake and the voice to moan and sob can help open many emotional and spiritual energy channels.

When was the last time you had a cry that was truly releasing?

Crying is a holistically human sound experience.

Crying is a sign that you are in touch with your soul. It is also a sign to others that you are present at the level of soul.

Someone suggested how wonderful it might be if, when the world leaders met, they could cry together for the pain of the world. For those moments at least, they would be in touch with their own spirit and the spirits of each other.

The Anatomy of Laughter

Laughter is another healing vibration of the soul. Experts have now confirmed what most everyone already knew intuitively: laughter can relieve stress.

In the average laugh, the diaphragm, thorax, abdomen, heart, lungs, and possibly even the liver get a brief workout. Dr. William Fry of Stanford University describes laughter as a kind of "stationary jogging." After Norman Cousins told the world, in his book

The Anatomy of an Illness, that he had laughed his way to recovery from a degenerative spinal condition, some doctors began to take a serious look at the healing potential of laughter.

Laughter has been known to clear foreign matter from the respiratory system, speed up circulation, and increase heart rate. It seems at times to be able to fight infection and alleviate hypertension.

The research hypothesis is that laughter stimulates the brain to produce hormones called catecholamines. These hormones may in turn trigger the release of endorphins, natural opiates that can reduce pain or discomfort from arthritis or allergies and from certain headaches and backaches.

If a laugh is especially vigorous, it flexes muscles in the face, arms, and legs. It sets the entire body vibrating, and sends happy sounds into the world.

The humor and joy implied in laughter helps relieve boredom, tension, guilt, depression, and anger. Laughter is considered a safe and socially acceptable sound, a civilized alternative to violence and noise.

According to Freud, laughter occurs when aggressive and angry energy is freed from repression. The more energy that is suddenly released, the louder and deeper the laughter.

The *Hara*-Laugh

If laughter has its physical and psychological components, it is also an expression of the human soul, or spirit. One can learn to laugh from the center of one's being. Such a laugh is called a *hara*-laugh. Al Huang, probably the most playful and provocative T'ai Ch'i master in the United States, can get even the most inhibited workshop participants vibrating with a liberating *hara*-laugh.

In Chinese calligraphy, Al Huang explains, laughter is depicted by a human with arms and legs flung outward, head up to the sky, everything "vibrating with mirth, like bamboo leaves in the wind." In his book *Quantum Soup: A Philosophical Entertainment*, he describes the way "to grow a proper laugh!" He begins with the analogy of a baby bamboo shoot pushing up through the earth.

"Start with just the thought of laughter," he writes. "Don't hurry it. Let it grow like the shoot. Wait for a genuine smile. Let it widen as a sound begins to tickle in the throat. Now let it begin to bounce around in the chest. Still, do not hurry it."

He then asks you to picture the rapidly growing bamboo stalk rising toward the sky, leaves rustling in the spring air.

"Allow your body to follow the leaves," he encourages, "expanding in all directions. Your breath is bigger, deeper, wider. Stretching. Let it grow. Watch it go. *Now* give it its sound."

The shoulders begin to shake, the belly begins to quiver. The sound coming from the center of the being escapes through the mouth. Like the bamboo sprout, it quakes and shakes and blows.

"Your very fingers are atingle with it," observes Al Huang. "Your toes and kneecaps and hips and lips become the very sound of laughter. It is everywhere."

Laughter is healthy soul food. It brings balance and harmony to the body, mind, and spirit. It is a blessing on the earth.

Sound and Spirit

In cultures less dominated by technology than ours, performance in music and dance at celebrations are not spectator events. Included in such cultural experiences are chanting, singing, drumming, and dancing. Everyone participates actively. Such ceremonies are used by all in the community to promote physical, emotional, and especially spiritual health. More specifically, participation in such music and movement promotes release of tension in mind and body, enjoyment and ecstasy, interpersonal and transpersonal communication.

For people in these cultures, sound and spirit are one. To make sound is to release spirit and energy.

Making Music

One of the simplest ways to get in touch with your own ability to release spiritual energy in music involves making music with the human voice, a musical instrument we all have. The voice has been used as a vehicle for spiritual uplifting and healing in every culture throughout history. It has been used professionally and ceremonially by shamans and medicine men, religious leaders and faith healers, minstrels and troubadors. Its functions are to heal, inspire, console, and establish contact with cosmic forces.

But anyone can learn to use the human voice in healing and spiritual ways, as any mother who has sung lullabies to her baby can attest.

The first step is to create a sound. Once you begin creating sounds, even with your own voice, you are a composer.

Composing music in this context is a dynamic form of meditation. But you do not need to know any formal laws of composition to get into the process. All that's required is a willingness to open your mouth and project a sound.

In workshops, we invite people to sing one sound on any pitch that they desire. Sometimes we ask them to explore a wide range of frequencies with a glissando—sliding up and down the scale—and find a tone that feels most comfortable and natural to them at the time.

Sliding up and down the scale also helps warm up the vocal chords and develops the voice's resonance. This exercise gives participants a chance to be more accurate in choosing a sound with which they feel comfortable.

A Single Sound

Singing one note is not a skill that people typically acquire, and yet it is perhaps one of the keys to successful composing and self-exploration.

The process of singing one note for an extended time brings about a number of chemical changes and metabolic processes in the body, including the possible release of endorphins in the brain as well as a mental concentration that allows the hemispheres to synchronize their functioning. The human voice is truly a magical vehicle for transformation.

One of the main differences between singing and talking is that singing emphasizes vowel sounds, while talking focuses on consonants. The so-called pure vowel sounds appear in similar spiritual and healing contexts throughout the world. For instance, the "ah" sound appears in the Sanskrit "Aum" chant, in the "Allah" of the

Middle East, and the "alleluia" and "Amen" of the Juedo-Christian traditions.

Each of the three pure vowel sounds are vibratory realities that are traditionally associated with particular attributes, energies, and parts of the body that resonate to the sound. According to the Sufis, an ancient near-Eastern mystery religion devoted to knowledge and enlightenment, the first vowel sound, "ah," signifies oneness or unity and radiates a golden color. It is an earth sound and is said to open the heart.

The second vowel, "oo" (as in soothing and cool), is generally considered to be a blue color. It is associates with water and relates to the throat. While "ah" seems to radiate energy, "oo" tends to draw energy inward.

The third pure vowel sound, "ee," is a more piercing sound associated with air and related to the mind. Its color is a bright blue-green, or turquoise.

Beyond the three pure vowel sounds are the "hmmm" (humming) and "oh" sounds. "Hmmm" is associated with the top of the head, and is said to produce all the colors of the rainbow. "Oh," as in go or so, is said to combine the breadth of "ah" and the depth of "oo."

Making Your Own Sound

The Sufis have explored the healing effects of sounds and music. They believe that certain sounds, along with their accompanying colors, affect us directly by means of the body's endocrine system. Those who know little about the Sufi methods of healing and less about the endocrine system can still tune into their own personal sound awareness.

Spend some time making sounds at different pitches (high, middle, low) and using different vowel sounds. Notice how the different sounds affect your body, mind and spirit.

There is a great need for songs and melodies that can be used to heal and balance energies. These might be songs to free the "child" in all of us, songs to ease emotional pain and spread joy, songs to open the heart and lift the spirit. Perhaps you might create one of them.

Take a moment and sing a melody. It can be one that you have heard before and like—or it can be one that you now "make up" for the first time.

By working primarily with pure tones and vowel sounds, making up simple melodies, you can go a long was to begin releasing energies within yourself. There are no harmful side effects to such music. It's totally free. There are no set rules. You really can't fail.

Even if you have been told in school that you did not have a good singing voice and had no musical ability, we say to you now: "You can create music that brings you joy and a sense of self-expression, *because it is already inside you just waiting to come out.*"

Testimony to Sound

Among people who have tried creating their own healing sounds, we get many positive reports.

"When I sing my own tones," wrote one, "I find a sensuous pleasure feeling the resonance of tones in my body. I like the way sound is transmitted back to the senses through my body."

"My voice has become more resonant since I started singing," said another, "and it affects my conversational voice, too."

"Singing my own music has not only freed my spirit in private," said another, "but my sense of freedom has carried over into self-expression in my relationships. Actually, I even find myself wanting to dance when I sing."

How wonderful it would be if such a holistic approach to using the human voice would become a part of the core curriculum in schools.

If we would only educate and develop each human voice in its potential to heal and inspire, this world would be a healthier, happier, and more loving place in which to live. We could uplift ourselves and those with whom we speak each time we speak.

Inside everyone there is a hidden musician waiting to get out. If

*you don't make music yourself, it is quite possible that you're
missing an important experience in your life.*

Begin With Simple Music

It is important to point out that we are not talking about creating
sophisticated, complex music. We are asking people to become involved in making music that, in one sense, takes no effort to listen
to or create.

Most symphonic, jazz, and even many rock compositions require
your conscious participation and attention in order to appreciate
their density of sound textures and layers of intricate harmonics
and counterpoint. In contrast, there is simple music—like a short
melody without words—that takes little effort to listen to or sing.

Nevertheless, such elemental music can be a deep and total experience. As you may have experienced in a simple chanting of
vowels on your favorite pitch, such a sound has a calming, centering
effect. It achieves this effect because it arises out of a calm and
centered place within you.

Releasing Spiritual Energy

Our lives are our music. Our every step is part of the cosmic
dance. Making our own music helps us become conscious of the
importance of our energy contribution to the great dance.

It is in this sense that the so-called primitive cultures participat-
ed in their community celebrations. With their voices and bodies
channeling the release of their spiritual energy, they entered into
the flow of that cosmic dance, often in order to restore balance and
harmony to their lives.

We are consciously focusing on very simple sounds—perhaps un-
interesting to the scientist—to help rediscover ancient methods of
using music and tone, vibrations and rhythms, and to learn how
they relate to spiritual and healing states of consciousness. The
connections to be made in this process are not between layers of
melody and harmony, but between the layers of energy available to
your life.

Simple Chanting

One of the most natural and most ancient sound forms, used by spiritual traditions in all ages to heal and energize, is chanting. Because of our intellectual fascination with intricacy and complexity in Western civilization, many simple Gregorian chant forms evolved into complex neumes and polyphony. They reached their height of complexity and sophistication in the late Middle Ages, in the cathedrals and monasteries of Europe. Such music was aesthetically stunning and was probably composed by spiritual giants, and its performance often required the talents of trained musicians.

The problem was that performance of these intricate musical tapestries required the fullest conscious attention. The singers could not afford to let their minds or spirits wander, lest they lose their place and perhaps mar the beauty and effectiveness of the piece.

This is not the kind of chant we are talking about here. There is another chant tradition preserved in both East and West that uses very short and simple melodic lines, with little or no harmony and few words.

The simplest of these is the "Om" (Aum) chant, which consists of a single, sustained note beginning with the lips shaping the "ah" sound, slowly changing to the "o" sound, and ending with the closed-lips "mmm" humming sound. After a relaxed inhalation, the chant is repeated. The "Aum" sound is made over and over, the process continuing for as long as you like.

For some, chanting "Aum" a dozen times is sufficient to put them in touch with the center of their being and the energy available to them. Others, who wish to enter deeper states of consciousness, may need to continue the chanting for ten minutes or longer.

Allowing the Sound

The point is not simply to make the "Aum" sound, but rather to allow the sound to carry you to the depths of your being, to the deepest sources of energy available to you. Let it carry you to that place where you connect with the energies of the universe, where you are in touch with the ground of your being, or where your soul meets God.

If you are new at chanting, the "Aum" chant is a good place to begin. It is easy to do, and is very powerful.

Please do not succumb to the temptation to move quickly to more sophisticated chants, especially if you are a professional musician.

Also, it is very easy to get caught up in technical awareness ("Isn't this clever?" or "Am I executing this phrase properly?") and lose the centered, spirit awareness that is the main purpose of the chant.

Chant Resources

If the "Aum" chant does not feel comfortable, perhaps you can choose some other single word or phrase that is powerful and meaningful to you. Some power words that people use for chanting include love, care, peace, one, God, Abba, Jesus, mercy, praise, hallelujah.

So sacred to Christians were the specific sounds of the Greek power words *Kyrie eleison* (Lord, have mercy) that even when the Church's language changed first to Latin and then to the vernacular, these chant words were kept in their original form.

Perhaps you will choose different chant words at different times. And you may choose to create different tones or melodies for your chants.

Louis Savary has created a cassette with two chants sung by the Dahlgren Chapel Choir at Georgetown University to help those new to chanting who would like the support of a group. On one side is the famous "Jesus Prayer." It was formulated by the monks on Mt. Athos in the sixth century, and popularized in the book *The Pilgrim*, the story of a holy man who is said to have recited the Jesus prayer continually throughout all the waking hours of his life.

On the other side of the cassette is a chant to the Divine Trinity. The Jewish tradition has created many beautiful chants, as have the Sufi, Hindu, and Buddhist traditions and certainly those of the various American Indian tribes. Among all these resources, you can find chants that feel right to you.

Holistic Toning

In Part I we described the practice called toning, clarified and explained by Laurel Elizabeth Keyes in her book *Toning: The Creative Power of the Voice.* There we presented toning as a practice to relax the body. But the experience is, in fact, more than physical.

According to Keyes, toning aids healing and fosters wholeness in a number of ways. First, it helps cleanse the energy fields surrounding you and others. Second, it invites the subconscious mind to cooperate with ideas held in the conscious mind. Third, it helps harmonize and balance the energies of the body, mind, and spirit.

Groaning in Spirit

Groaning itself can be an expression of the human spirit. It is also a biblical form of praying. For example, it was used by the writer of the Psalms, by some of the prophets, by Paul the Apostle, and by Jesus.

When the Israelites were held captive in Egypt, it was their groaning that touched God in a special way. The psalmist and the prophets prayed with groans and sighs, especially during times of intense shame, grief, sorrow, misery, and oppression.

For thousands of years, until this day, the Jewish people have carried on the tradition of lamentation, crying out to God at the Wailing Wall at the western side of the Temple in Jerusalem.

Just before Jesus cured the deaf man from Sidon, the Bible says that Jesus looked up to heaven, groaned, and then said to the man, "Ephphatha." ("Be opened.") (Mark 7:34) Jesus' groan was part of his healing prayer.

Twice during the events surrounding Lazarus' death, Jesus spontaneously groaned in what appeared to be a way of centering himself before his prayer to God to bring Lazarus back to life. (John 11:33, 38) Various translations of this passage describe this act of

Jesus as "groaning within himself," "groaning in the Spirit," "being deeply moved in Spirit," and "with a sigh that came straight from the heart." There is no question that Jesus' groaning was a prayerful, spiritual act.

Paul the Apostle, writing to the Romans, describes not only humans, but also the entire cosmos in a groaning prayer of eager longing. "The whole creation," Paul wrote, "has been groaning in travail together until now, groaning to be released from pain and suffering; and on that day the world around us will share in the glorious freedom which we as God's children will enjoy."

Paul recommends that we groan not only because of pain and suffering, but also because we wish and desire new life and wholeness.

The Next Step in Toning

After the period of groaning, explains Laurel Keyes, you will find that the voice is inclined to rise, like a siren. Perhaps it will drop back and rise again, over and over, until it reaches the tone that feels right. When you find the right tone, keep toning.

A toning session may last ten minutes or an hour.

When your being feels cleansed, a sigh is released. This is the signal that your inner spirit is satisfied. Usually at this time you will feel good, perhaps even joyful, confident, or free. At this moment, your entire being is cleansed and open.

Keyes recommends finding something to fill the cleansed spiritual vessel—perhaps sitting quietly in meditation, singing a favorite song, reading a poem or a biblical passage, welcoming grace or light into yourself.

She never tires of reiterating her basic belief: "You can create a new world for yourself through the power of your voice."

Focusing Spiritual Energies

The voice can be used—through procedures such as chanting and toning—to unify and focus the forces available to us. It is possible with such spiritual energies to be creative, to change our environment, to be healed, to heal others, to make life useful and joyful.

Humans seem to be the only creatures capable of changing their lives through imagination and choice. The human spirit is our inheritance and we are invited to claim it.

Your life deserves to be sung.

Chapter 16

SOUND WITHIN

The "Within"

We are a civilization coming to maturity. One sign of this is that we are beginning to become aware of the inner journey.

Theologian and paleontologist Pierre Teilhard de Chardin said that all matter had not only a "without" (an external visible and tangible quality that could be measured and studied), but also a "within" (an invisible, intangible spiritual quality that was probably not the proper domain of scientific measurement and scrutiny).

Poet Gerard Manley Hopkins felt that many poets described the outward landscape of the world. He attempted, in the concepts, rhythms, and sounds of his poems, to describe its "inscape."

Music has a "without" and a "within." It has both audible and inaudible sounds. To experience music fully, both kinds of sounds need to be "heard."

Music, too, has its outer landscape in the technical arrangement of notes into melodies, rhythms, harmonies, and so forth which are fascinating and beautiful when studied on the manuscript page or heard performed in the concert hall. But music also has its "inscape," the inner reality that plays out in our imaginations, feelings, body, and spirit.

Sound is one of the holy gifts, a holy communion.

Things Most People Never Hear

A few years ago, Byrd Taylor and Peter Parnall created a book for children called *The Other Way to Listen*. The book tells about two young people who not only learned to listen but also found a new relationship to the living world of nature.

When you know "the other way to listen," you begin to hear things most people never hear—like wildflowers bursting open, rocks murmuring, or mountains singing. Once you learn how to do it, it seems like the most natural thing in the world.

"Of course, it takes a lot of practice," explains one of the book's characters, "and you can't be in a hurry. In fact, most people never hear those things at all."

Learning to Hear

Novelist Andy Stone created a fantasy story called *Song of the Kingdom*, which tells about a young apprentice musician who learned to hear the within of things. Here is a piece of dialogue between Orin, the apprentice, and Oban, his master teacher.

"I don't want you to think about this (instrumental) music yet. There's music all around you that you have to hear first: the music of the stream, the music of the forest."

"I know the music of the forest, master, the sound of the wind in the branches."

"No, boy, that's part of the music of the wind. The music of the forest isn't something you hear in quite the same simple way. It's there all the time, whether the wind is blowing or not. It is the spirit of the forest, the song of the life of the woods. It is a song of being. Everything has such a song, the music it makes by existing. The stream has its song whether it's flowing or frozen. The wind has its song even when it's still."

Oban the master told Orin that if he listened in the right way he could hear all these songs, and even the song of his own life, "the music of your days and moments."

Oban told Orin to listen to the song of his life, even to himself as he carried drinking water from the stream and chopped firewood.

The pupil told his master that he was certain he would never hear any such music at all.

Oban replied that as a musician, he had to learn to listen before he would be able to hear, and he would have to hear before he could ever play his instrument.

"Stop thinking about anything you've heard before," Oban explained. "What most people hear is only the least part of what there is to be heard.

If you expect the songs of the world to crowd in on you like the songs of the birds in the woods, you'll never hear them at all. How will you find anything new when you expect it to be nothing more than you already know? Don't make rules for the music to follow. Just listen. Listen." (Andy Stone, *Song of the Kingdom*, New York: Doubleday, 1979.)

The Magic of Music

Is all this talk about inner music just part of a sweet fairy tale? The product of a creative and fertile imagination? Some form of verbal magic?

Let us peek beyond the metaphor, beyond the parable.

Music is magical indeed. It is everyday magic. It is magic that everyone can perform. It is the magic of life.

Is it not magical that certain sounds can make people get up and dance, or sing, or cry, or go off to fight for a cause, or evoke feelings of love and tenderness?

Is it not magical that certain music can relax tensions, initiate healing, restore friendship, release anger, build courage?

Is it not magical that certain music can evoke the presence of God, engender a sense of communion with nature, release archetypal energies, foster meditation, alter consciousness, and call us to our highest purpose in life?

If music is so magically powerful, then a musical instrument in the wrong hands can be potentially a more dangerous instrument than an axe. (Perhaps not coincidentaly, many contemporary musicians refer to their instrument as their axe. Might this be telling us something?)

Exploring the Gift of Music

That music and musicians are potentially powerful forces is no reason to abandon music. It is reason to embrace and explore the world of music to its fullest potential.

Even though music can be used to delight and entertain, it is not a mere plaything, but very clearly a gift of God.

According to Greek mythology, Orpheus was given a lyre by the god Apollo and was instructed in its use by the muses (hence the term "music"). For Orpheus, music was a means of worshiping the gods. And, according to the myth, with music he possessed the power to move and enchant humans, beasts, trees, and even rocks.

We might begin to understand what Orpheus was able to do by reminding ourselves, as contemporary scientists have done, that everything in the universe, both animate and inanimate, is vibrational in nature.

It doesn't require a great leap of faith to see that the humans, beasts, trees, and rocks of the Orpheus legend were conglomerates of vibrating atoms and molecules, and that these vibrating elements could in turn be set into other modes of motion by sound stimuli.

Even before the strings of Orpheus' lyre were plucked to make an audible sound, those strings—the atoms and molecules in them— were vibrating with incredible velocity. A well-known chemist from Johns Hopkins University, Dr. Donald H. Andrews, wrote in his book called *The Symphony of Life*, that "if we but had the right ears, we could hear these atoms humming and singing."

The Spiritual Dimension

But the inner music is more than just atoms vibrating, as Orpheus knew. There is a spiritual and divine dimension to it.

"Music is moral law," wrote Plato. "It is the essence of order and leads to all that is good, just, and beautiful, of which it is the invisible, but nevertheless dazzling, passionate, and eternal form."

Plato talks about music in the realm of celestial vibrations and divine archetypes. Many other wise humans have been at home with this spiritual language of music. The list reads like a Who's Who of all time, and includes Pythagoras, Plotinus, Martin Luther, Kierkegaard, Carlyle, Verdi, Mozart, Brahms, Scriabin, and Beethoven.

Sufi philosopher Al-Ghazali wrote, "The purpose of music, considered in relation to God, is to arouse longing for Him and passionate love toward Him and to produce states in which He reveals Himself." (These states are called "ecstasy" by the Sufis.)

Music has had, and can have, a divine purpose. Today, great music is common and easily available to all. While music can be a reflection of a higher order of reality, in the depths of our consciousness each of us inhabits this inner world of spiritual being.

Obviously, not all the sound and music that we hear qualifies as spiritually profound. How are we to distinguish the levels of depth in musical composition?

Blake's Fourfold Vision

In the poem "Now I a Fourfold Vision See," composed in 1802, William Blake presented his version of an ancient truth; that there are four stages of understanding, or levels of meaning. The four forms (or visions, in Blake's terminology), have been applied to poetry, literature, biblical texts, and so forth. In these four levels, people have found analogies to orders of imagination, levels of creativeness, states of consciousness, and structures of formal logic.

In his profound article "Music and Fourfold Vision" (*ReVision*, 1983) psychology professor Joel Funk suggests that Blake's fourfold vision has its counterpart in the general structural characteristics of classical Western music.

Single Vision

Blake's *single vision*, or first level of perception, is limited to what physical eyesight enables us to see. It reflects the world of consensus opinion as to what is real. Thus a cloud is a cloud, a desk is a desk, an inkblot is an inkblot. Single vision is very literal-meaning.

When an artist or composer produces works of single vision, explains Funk, "the product will simply repeat existing forms with perhaps some minor degree of variation."

Such composers are still imbedded in the current cultural system and do not question its authority. Much popular music, folk music, country and western, blues, and rock fits the single vision category; as do many typical Christian hymns, which may aspire to the spiritual in content, but musically are quite linear and time-bound.

Funk suggests that Beethoven's first piano compositions, written at age twelve, and which were never given an opus number, were of this first level.

Twofold Vision

Blake's *twofold vision* witnesses the first manipulation of imagination, a recognition of an allegorical meaning that lies beneath the surface meaning. Thus a cloud formation may be seen as sheep grazing or the face of a well-known political figure; an inkblot might represent two dancers, two students, or two monks in prayer.

Notice how the imagery is still bound by existing stereotypes. There is no smashing of cultural boundaries, nothing genuinely new.

Some musical examples might include a few popular musical selections that are a bit off the common track, for example, David Rose's *The Syncopated Clock* and the *Trumpeter's Holiday* or Michel Legrand's *What Are You Doing the Rest of Your Life*?

Classically, Funk suggests that Beethoven's early piano sonatas and string quartets would exemplify twofold vision.

Threefold Vision

Threefold vision goes beyond the given, even beyond the cultural imagination. The artist of threefold vision is a truly conscious creator for the first time. Regions outside the conscious ego have begun to be tapped. Signs of spontaneity and a relaxation of control are evident in the artistic work, but the work "still remains on *this* side of the transpersonal, although occasional peak experiences may afford glimpses of higher states."

According to Funk, Beethoven's *Eroica Symphony* and most of his "second period" works reflect threefold vision.

"Whereas works of single and twofold vision can be created by skill alone," explains Funk, "music on the threefold vision level requires the participation of unconscious processes and hence cannot be convincingly 'faked.' "

Each threefold-level composition bears a distinctive character so that, once you clearly understand it, it appears quite unlike any other composition, even those of the same composer.

Some have called threefold-level music Orphic music. It seems to transcend standard elements such as linearity, theme and development, harmonic progression, and personal emotionality. Orphic music uses structures more suited to a nonlinear, timeless, blissful mode of being.

Fourfold Vision

Fourfold vision is still a step beyond. It is an intense transpersonal vision characteristic of the mystic, the seer, the prophet. Its emotions are archtypally powerful—horror, awe, ecstasy, desolation, unity. It operates in the realm of the soul.

At this level, the composer surrenders to a higher agency. When asked how he composed, Mozart is said to have responded, "God speaks to me and I write." Brahms, Beethoven, and many others have made essentially the same claim.

Beethoven's magnificent *Missa Solemnis* is an example of a work at this stage. It is devoid of all cultural imagery and devoid of all dualism in which self and world might appear separate. Funk lists in this category "Scriabin's *Poem of Ecstasy*, Bruckner's *Great Mass*, Bach's *Mass in B Minor*, Mahler's *Eighth Symphony*, Fauré's *Requiem*, Strauss' *Death and Transfiguration*, Pachelbel's *Canon in D*, and Mozart's *Requiem*. He also mentions works of Wagner, Bloch, Morales, Victoria, Delius, Hovhaness, Ravel, Debussy, Vaughn Williams, Palestrina, Gesualdo, Ives, Holst, and Messaien.

New Age Music and Fourfold Vision

While Funk feels that New Age composers have produced music that "is indeed quite beautiful, relaxing, peaceful, even sometimes heavenly," he still feels a "lingering disquiet" that much of this music is not really transcendent and transpersonal.*

It seems evident, however, that music composed in the threefold and fourfold levels is capable of releasing higher energies. Composers, performers, and listeners who are comfortable at the fourfold level demonstrate that the "within" of such music offers a magnificent "inscape" for those who are ready for the spiritual journey.

"The masterpieces of those composers gifted with fourfold vision open us up to the radiance of being," concludes Joel Funk. "Listening to their works, we are transported to unseen realms, and are, temporarily at least, made whole."

---

*I was surprised and delighted to discover that Funk listed my *Zodiac Suite* among compositions having fourfold vision. I have always known that there is much more to this music than simply a relaxation response. I believe that Dr. Funk has tapped into a higher order of criticism that provides us with a glimpse into the hidden aspects of this, and much other, music.

Chapter 17

SOUND MEDITATION

"Realizing God"

"The use of music for spiritual attainment and healing of the soul, which was prevalent in ancient times," wrote Sufi Master Hazrat Inayat Khan in *The Mysticism of Sound* (1979), "is not found to the same extent now. Music has been made a pastime, the means of forgetting God instead of realizing God."

There has been a rising interest in meditation over the past decade. However, many contemporary meditators do not seem directly interested in realizing God. Instead, some focus on meditation as a form of relaxation and a way to deal with stress. Others see meditation primarily as a kind of preventive medicine, or as a gateway to clearer thinking and creativity. Still others meditate to get ideas for books, articles, sermons, lectures, and workshops.

While all of these reasons for meditating are acceptable, it is clear that the fundamental reason for meditation in all the spiritual traditions of the world is to be present to Being. That Being might be the meditator's soul, the soul or spirit of others, the spirit of God, the ground of life, or all of the above.

The feelings and inner movement traditionally associated with meditation are spiritual ones such as peace, joy, love, faith, unity, praise, gratitude, and the like. It has been said that one meditator balances out a hundred angry people.

Appropriate music may be used to facilitate a shift of consciousness into the meditative state, where spiritual affective responses are likely. An aural environment may be created to help individual meditators get in touch with the soul as an integral part of the whole self.

When you are in touch with your own soul, the awareness of God is not far away.

Sacred Music

Music and the presence of God have long been associated. Not only do we find the great composers using religious themes and texts as the basis of their compositions as in the great masses and requiems, but even at a very primitive level sounds and the divine are often associated.

While some of these are nature sounds such as the ocean's roar, the wind's howling, and the thunderclap, others are human-made sounds such as the bell or gong.

Meditation With Music

In all cultures, people have used music to facilitate meditation and religious experience. Some of this music is composed primarily for communal worship and celebration, some of it is composed primarily for personal sacred time. In each case, the music is designed to deepen and intensify the spiritual experience.

We have learned some ways to help music do what it was designed to do for those following a spiritual path. Here are some simple guidelines for doing meditation with music in whatever style you choose to use.

Before beginning the music, take a comfortable position and grow quiet in body, mind and spirit. (Most people have their favorite ways of getting relaxed and growing quiet, such as taking a few deep breaths or stretching.)

Realize that you are in the presence of your own soul and of God. Acknowledge that what you are doing is a sacred act. Be grateful ahead of time for the gift of the music and the energies that it may release in you. Now, simply allow yourself to surrender to the music without being critical of the performance or the record's quality.

While the music is playing, let go completely. Feel the music flowing over you and into you. Open yourself to the healing and energizing vibrations that enter you.

Let your body enjoy the music, let your imagination respond actively to the sound stimulus, and let your spirit be carried by the music wherever it needs to go.

When the music is over, remain quiet for a few minutes, reviewing what happened in your body, your imagination, your emotions, and your spirit.

Many people who meditate with music like to keep a journal to note important elements of the experience. Others may prefer to draw some image or feeling from the meditation. Still others may enjoy dancing or moving in reverent ways to express what happened during the meditation time.

The point is that if a gift of energy, awareness, healing, insight, or relationship was given to you during meditation, find a way to bring that gift back into ordinary consciousness so that it may continue to delight and benefit you and others.

Accepting Gifts

The left side of our brain tends to function by perceiving the world in a linear manner. It does not know how to deal well with gifts or even to appreciate them properly, because its proper function is to label and organize the input it receives into separate and discrete categories. It operates logically and rationally. The left hemisphere by itself is often quite out of its depth in meditation.

In contrast, the emotive and imaginative right hemisphere tends to accept what is given to it more freely. Not only does it welcome gifts, but it perceives them in wider patterns; it has the capacity for re-cognition.

A frequent gift in meditation comes by way of the imagination in the form of an image, symbol, gesture, or color. The simplest gift is one of color.

Meditation and Color

Light and all its composite colors are expressed in vibrations. If we put colors in musical language, the harmonics of color are about 40 octaves higher than audible sound.

For example, vibrations at 1000 cycles per second are easily audible. If you double the vibrations to 2000 cycles per second, that's one octave higher. If you double it again to 4000 cycles per second, that's another octave. A normal piano spans a bit more than seven octaves. If, hypothetically, we could extend the piano keyboard another 35 or 50 octaves higher, the keys at the higher end would produce colors—rather than audible sounds—when played.

The colors that we have around us seem to affect the whole person—not only our bodies and minds, but our spirits as well. For this reason, in meditating for wholeness and striving for the highest in ourselves, light, color, and sound can have a strong impact.

Although there are many ways to integrate meditation, music, and color, we offer only a few here as suggested starting places. You may want to create your own special ways to use music and color in your spiritual growth. You will find enough basic information in this book and the references given in the last section to create scores of procedures and techniques to use.

One of the simplest ways of tuning into the potential of activating the sound and color synergistic effect is to focus on the seven main energy centers that have been known to exist in and around the body. In the East, these have been traditionally known as the chakras. In the West, they have also been known by that name. More recently, doctors such as William McGarey of the A.R.E. Medical Center refer to them as "neuro-hormonal transducers."

But whatever we call them, scientific instrumentation has measured significant changes in energy potential on the surface of the skin in the areas precisely where the ancient yogis and Chinese acupuncturists indicated that there was a major, spiritual energy center. For our purposes, it is enough to consider that each of these energy centers is associated with a specific tone of the musical scale and with a specific color of the rainbow.

It will be furthermore noted that there is a correspondence between the seven-member scale of musical tones, the seven-member scale of colors of the rainbow, and the seven spiritual energy centers. It seems more than coincidence that there is a one-to-one relationship on these different octaves of reality.

I have found that the sound and color resonance extends beyond the specific energy center to the area of the body in a horizontal plane surrounding that area. Even getting close to the mark, in other words, will still evoke a positive response. In this paradigm, the combined openness to color, sound, and the energy centers is intended to welcome and channel the appropriate energy.

Steven Halpern's Spectrum Meditation

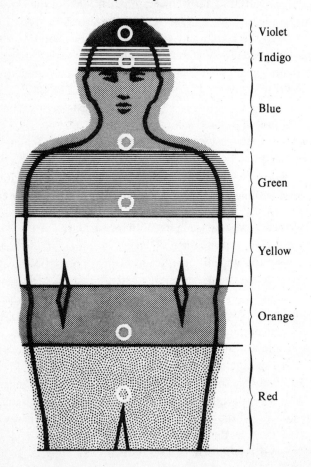

The Spectrum Meditation

The music specifically designed for this exercise is the *Spectrum Suite*.

To prepare for this meditation, take a comfortable posture in which the spine is straight—either sitting, standing, or lying on your back.

Take a few relaxed, deep breaths and let yourself relax even more.

Then let the music begin.

As the music plays, do not attempt to analyze or anticipate the musical structure, but simply allow your body, mind, and spirit to float with the sound. You might imagine the music washing over you, or massaging you.

The recording is divided into seven sections, each about three minutes in length. During the first selection, which has the keynote C, allow your attention to focus around the base of your spine, the first spiritual energy center. Hear and feel the tones of this selection resonating in that area and imagine, if you wish, vibrations of pure red bathing this area of your body, filling you with the energy to transmit life.

When the second selection comes on, with the keynote D, begin to raise your focus of attention to the second energy center, below your navel. Use your imagination to help you. Experience the vitality of the orange color and the energy of self affirmation it brings.

At the third selection, keynote E, focus upon the area around the solar plexus. Visualize the color yellow, and open yourself to the energies of courage and forgiveness, including self-forgiveness.

When the fourth selection comes on, keynote F, focus upon the heart area. Let yourself be bathed in green as you welcome the energy of unconditional love, for yourself and others.

When the fifth selection begins, keynote G, visualize the color sky blue around the throat. Welcome the energy of will power into your life.

When the sixth selection begins, keynote A, focus at the center of your forehead. See the area bathed in depeest blue, and be open to the grace of wisdom.

When the seventh and final selection begins, keynote B, focus your attention at the crown of your head. Visualize a violet color there and welcome the energy of divine consciousness.

When the music concludes, allow yourself to remain in this elevated state for a few more minutes. Enjoy the reality of your spiritual nature. Express your gratitude in any way that seems appropriate.

When you are ready to return to ordinary waking consciousness, you will probably feel relaxed and refreshed.

This spiritual energy bath may be taken in the morning, the evening, or anytime you feel a need for it. Many people have made it a daily practice.

At those times when you don't have access to the music or the twenty minutes required for the full meditation, I have found it useful to do a mini-spectrum attunement. This can be done in the same sequence, but in a total of two minutes, using the powers of your mind to focus the appropriate energy—whether you have the soundtrack or not. Clearly, the impact is not quite as intense or effective, but a little bit of attunement is better than none at all.

Another variation of this meditation, with a more religious orientation, correlates the seven energy centers with the seven petitions of The Lord's Prayer. This Centering Meditation was produced on cassette, with music by Steven Halpern and narration by Louis Savary.

Preparing for Silence

Although the experience of music can accompany a powerful spiritual experience, there may be times for meditation and prayer when you will want to be totally silent.

At such times, however, you may use music to *prepare* you for the deep silence, music that will quiet your body andmind and open your spirit to be present to the divine.

Such musical pieces are very special. When you discover those that best prepare you for true silence, keep a list of them and use them often. As your body and mind grow used to these pieces, they will learn to respond more and more quickly, and spontaneously produce the desired quiet state.

Silence

"Silence is the great revealer," says Lao Tsu. To receive the revelation that silence gives, you must first immerse yourself in it.

Silence is not merely the absence of noise or sound, it is a positive and specific state of consciousness.

It is not easy to attain the state of silence, as the spiritual teachers remind us. Yet, for almost everyone, silence seems to be a necessary prerequisite to higher forms of prayer and meditation.

In our noisy culture, it is seemingly impossible to close the outer ears, quiet the constantly wandering mind, and still the incessant turmoil of heart. Silence is not a desideratum in our day. Many who approach a deep silence find it frightening, so they panic and flee.

In contemporary literature, according to R. Murray Schafer in *The Tuning of the World*, who researched references to sound and silence in published works, there are few happy descriptions of silence.

"The modifiers of 'silence' used most recently," he writes, "are solemn, oppressive, deathlike, numb, weird, awful, gloomy, brooding, eternal, painful, lonely, heavy, despairing, stark, suspenseful, aching, alarming."

This is not the silence of peace, contentment, fulfillment. This is not the silence that is the gateway to the divine presence.

Many contemporary writers seem not to have tasted the silence that reveals union at the core on one's being—union with God, union with others, union with the whole world.

Writing of silence, the Indian mystic Kirpal Singh said, "When there is no sound, it is said that there is no hearing, but that does not mean that hearing has lost its preparedness. Indeed, when there is no sound, hearing is most alert, and when there is sound the hearing nature is least developed."

When there is no audible sound, the soul is most alert for the inaudible vibrations of the universe.

When there is no audible sound, the soul is most alert for the voice of God.

In silence, the soul is most ready to hear.

Music Heard and Unheard

Is it possible that certain *music itself* can effect an effortless elevation of consciousness to spiritual realms? Can music itself help spiritually transform a community or a culture?

Is it possible that certain archetypal combinations of frequencies and resonances can trigger genetically preprogrammed responses that can purify, sensitize, and uplift listeners?

Is it possible that such combinations can be learned and used by composers and performers to stimulate energies of unselfish love, caring, cooperation, a sense of justice, and a desire for peacefully productive human relationships?

And even if such music were able to be composed, would we be fully able to hear it, that is, could we ingest it with body, mind, and soul?

At some level of being, we all know there is a music beyond us, waiting to be heard. We know that it is capable of being heard. And yet so few, even reportedly, hear it.

Perhaps very few are listening.

Like Orin the pupil, we need a master musician like Oban to remind us:

If you expect the Song of the Kingdom to crowd in on you like the sound of the birds in the woods, you will never hear it at all. How will you hear anything new if you expect it to be nothing more than what you already know? Don't make rules for the music to follow. Just listen. Listen.

Perhaps listening is the key.

Once, when a violinist complained to Beethoven that a cadenza he wrote was impossible to execute, the great composer was reported to have said, "How can I be concerned about your human limitations when I am trying to speak to my God?"

Perhaps in our generation we have less need to speak to God than to begin listening to God.

When sound meditation is true to itself, it calls us to listen in ways that transcend cultural limitations. It invites us to listen to God, to the eternal Song of the Kingdom.

But what would be characteristic of such divine music?

Any sounds made by God would have been initiated before our birth, would have continued unabated and unchanging throughout our lifetime, and would extend beyond our death.

Such a sound, as Schafer observes, would be perceived by us as *silence*.

This is not the silence of an empty vacuum, but the positive and full silence of the eternal music.

Can such silence be heard?

Yes.

PART FOUR

Sound Helps

SOFTWARE AND HARDWARE

Sound Software

Records and Cassettes for General Healthful Listening

It has become axiomatic to note that "one person's passion may be another person's poison." As with most music, there is no foolproof way to predict whether or not you will enjoy a particular recording of this "alternative music."

The problem of recommending specific selections for your healthful listening pleasure is complicated by the fact that, in many cases, a recording artist may produce one tape that is excellent for our purposes, another one that is fine for other forms of enjoyment, and perhaps even another that shouldn't have been released at all.

So what is a listener to do? There are several inexpensive ways to begin. Ask your friends if they have any recommendations in this regard. You might be surprised to find out that some of them are quite familiar with this music. Often people will hesitate to share this new music with others, lest they be thought too "far out."

You might listen for music of this kind on radio. Around the country there are a growing number of programs, pioneered by Stephen Hill and Anna Turner's "Music from the Heart of Space." Typically, they are found late at night and usually on PBS; but, as more listeners request this at primetime, the availability of such music on the air cannot help but increase.

A third possibility would be to check out the music media sections in holistically oriented magazines, such as *New Age Journal* or *Yoga Journal.* You might also consider writing your local newspaper and asking them to do a feature article on New Age music.

There is nothing "far out" about most of this music. It is just "other" than the prevailing orientation of most music that we have already been exposed to. Twenty years from now, this music may well be considered to be the contemporary "classical" music of the 1980s.

In their day, writers criticized Beethoven, Wagner, and Stravinsky for destroying "classical" music. In hindsight, of course, we recognize that these composers represented new directions, not destruction. The same may be said for much of the music we describe in this book.

Already, several major record chains, such as Tower Records and the Wherehouse, are stocking this new music in their stores. Many independent record shops in your area may also have some. If not, request that they begin to carry a selection.

When I began my own record company in 1975, I had much more success in introducing my recordings into stores that were concerned more with a holistic lifestyle, such as health food stores and bookstores, than with record stores. Many such stores now carry a fine selection of recordings. Some of them even let you listen to your selection in the store before you buy it. If yours doesn't, request that they do.

Another new development is the rise of shops that are designed purely for listening. About the size of a large van, these shops feature personal stereo systems, so that you can audition whichever tape you want.

You can also get a firsthand sample of the music by checking out holistic health fairs, environmental conferences, and the like. Many of these include a booth devoted to the new music.

By and large, however, the most extensive selection is available by mail. When I sent out my first catalog in 1976, I had the field to myself. Now, a whole host of alternatives are available. Following my lead, some of the companies even offer money-back guarantees, so that if the music does not deliver what the advertising promises, you, the customer, are not stuck with an unwelcome addition to your library.

A point to consider is that none of these "one-stop" record and tape catalogs can do justice in the limited amount of space to any individual artist. If you enjoy someone's work, write to the address listed on the liner notes. Let the artist know how you feel, especially if you are requesting a free catalog of their other work.

Speaking as someone who gets an opportunity to read many such letters, I can tell you that receiving positive response is one of the most fulfilling aspects of the work. So keep those cards and letters coming!

The Alternative Top-40

To get your own collection of recordings underway, you might check the full catalogs of the musicians themselves or their distributors for more details.

New artists are debuting all the time. There is no easy way for anyone to keep up with the mushrooming growth of the field. On the other hand, because of the nature of the music, the recordings don't "get old" in the same way that a Top-40 song will. You can listen to many of these recordings over and over, year after year.

Each of the following artists has a number of recordings to his or her credit. Some may suit you better than others, but each artist offers a unique vision of the new horizons of music.

For Meditation and Relaxation and Listening Pleasure

Kitaro: *Silk Road* (Canyon Records)
Steven Halpern: *Dawn* (Halpern Sounds)
Paul Horn: *Inside* (Golden Flute)
Iasos: *Interdimensional Music* (Interdimensional Music)
Emerald Web: *Valley of the Birds* (BobKat Productions)
Deuter: *Haleakala* (Kuckuck Records)
Georgia Kelly: *Seapeace* (Heru Records)
Paul Winter: *Common Ground* (Living Music Records)
William Aura: *Auramusic* (William AuraMusic)

Mark Allen and Friends: *Summer Suite* (Rising Sun)
Dallas Smith: *Stellar Voyage* (Rising Sun)
Schawkie Roth: *You are the Ocean* (Heaven on Earth)
Daniel Kobialka: *Timeless Motion* (Li-sem)
Michael Stearns: *Morning Jewel* (Continuum Montage)
Paul Warner: *Waterfall Music* (Waterfall Music Records)
Environments: *Ultimate Seashore* (Atlantic)
Solitudes: *Spring Morning on the Prairies* (Solitudes)
George Winston: *Autumn* (Windham Hill)

Catalogs: Access to Tools

Halpern Sounds, 1775 Old County Road #9, Belmont, CA 94002.
Mystical Rose Books and Tapes, P.O. Box 38, Malibu, CA 90265.
Narada Distributing, 1804 E. North Avenue, Milwaukee, WI 53202.
P.E.P. Distributors, 630 Skyview Drive, West Carrollton, OH 45449.
Source Distributing and New Age Co-op, P.O. Box 1207, Carmel Valley, CA 93924.
Vital Body Marketing, 42 Orchard Street, Manhassett, NY 11030.

Meditation Music with Spoken Narrations

Tom Budzynski: *Relaxation*, Futurehealth, 2133 Bristol Pike, Bensalem, PA 19020. Send for catalog.
Steven Halpern: *The Joy of Learning* (With Harmonic Affirmations®), 1775 Old County Road #9, Belmont, CA 94002. Send for catalog.
Linda Keiser and Louis Savary: *Healing Through Mary in Music*, Credence Cassettes #A 1551. ($7.95)
Emmett E. Miller, M.D.: *Letting Go of Stress*, 945 Evelyn, Menlo Park, CA 94025. Send for catalog.
Louis Savary: *Biblical Meditations with Music I, II,* Credence Cassettes #A312, A313. (Each $7.95)
   A Centering Meditation on the Lord's Prayer, music composed by Steven Halpern, Credence Cassettes #A394. ($7.95)

Self-Actualization I, II, Credence Cassettes #A314, A315. (each $7.95)

Theresa Scheihing: *Centering Meditations with Music: The Beautiful Earth*, Credence Cassettes, a three-cassette album AA1454. ($24.95)

Brad and Francie Steiger: *Starbirth Odyssey*, Harmonious Books, 7725 East Redfield, Suite 101, Scottsdale, AZ 85260. Send for catalog.

Dick Sutphen: *Blossoming Rose* (Superconscious Symbol Meditation). See Mystical Rose catalog, Box 38, Malibu, CA 90265.

Music and Videos and Television

Combining uplifting music with uplifting visuals is a natural marriage. As of this writing, we are finally witnessing the availability of a limited number of items of software to grace your video-cassette recorder and television screen. We can expect to see more broadcasting of such eye-and-ear food on the cable stations, and public television. You may even see it on the major networks before long. Many of these videotapes use optical- and video-generated imagery, mandalas, and laser lights and scenes from nature coupled with the music to create an experience of "visual music."

Beck, Stephen. *Illuminated Music.* Electron Video Creations, 41 Tunnel Rd., Berkeley, CA 94705

Emerald Web: *Photonos*, see Sutphen, Mystical Rose Catalog, Box 38, Malibu, CA 90265.

Steven Halpern and David Fortney: *HTV: Summer Wind*, Anti-Frantic Music Video, Halpern Sounds, 1775 Old County Road #9, Belmont CA 94002.

Iasos: *Crystal Vista*, Inter-Dimensional Video, P.O. Box 594, Waldo Point, Sausalito, cA 94965.

Ken Jenkins: *Beauty*, Immediate Future Productions, 531 Benvenue Avenue, Los Altos, CA 94022.

PBS Television: In conjunction with the Grace Foundation under executive producer William Neil, PBS is producing three educational films on sound and hearing: *To Hear* (1983), *The Hurt that Does Not Show* (1984), and *Noise, the Invisible Menace* (1985).

Walsh, Mary. *Enchanted Landscapes, Vol. I, II & IV*. P.O. Box 1341, Los Altos, CA 94022.

Sound Hardware

Helps for the Hearing-Impaired

"IR (Infra Red) Personal Hearing System," Audio Devices Inc., 4702 East Calle del Medio, Phoenix, AZ 85018.

"Phonic Ear Personal FM System," Phonic Ear, Inc., 250 Camino Alto, Mill Valley, CA 94941.

See also *EPA Journal*, October 1979 issue; and *Shhh Magazine*, especially January/February and July/August 1982 issues.

For Masking Sounds

Omnitronics Retreat. Ten-minute electronic relaxer; pink and white sound to relieve stress and tension. Mystical Rose Catalog.

Earth Resonance Generator, by Pat Flanagan. This device produces a pulsating electromagnetic field at 8–10 cycles per second, which is useful in counteracting the efects of electromagnetic smog. Flanagan Research Ltd., P.O. Box 686, Novato, CA 94948.

Life Field Polarizer. A white, cone-shaped device that correctly repolarizes the electrical current in your house when placed on any active wire. Environmental Polarity Research, P.B. Box 22528, San Diego CA 92122.

EDUCATION AND TRAINING

Sound Education

Quiet School Materials
U.S. Environmental Protection Agency
ONAC* ANR-471
Washington, D.C. 20469
Materials for elementary schools

The following are from Donna McCord Dickman, available from:
E.R.I.C. Document Repro Services
P.O. Box 190
Arlington, VA 22210
703/841-1212

Preparing for a Quieter Tomorrow (junior and senior high school
teacher guide)
ED-201 508
SE-034 853

Sounds Alive: A Noise Workbook (for elementary school)
ED-201 509
SE-034 854

Sounds Alive: A Noise Workbook, Teacher's Guide
ED-201 510
SE-034 055

---

*ONAC: Office of Noise Abatement and Control

Operation SHHH

This program teaches children about noise. It involves teacher
guides, student workbooks, activity charts, color posters of
Shherman, and the stoplight sound meter. Program cost:
$500.00.
SHHH
4848 Battery Lane, Suite 100
Bethesda, MD 20814

Self-Help in Action: Special Report

Free. Contact:
SHHH
4848 Battery Lane, Suite 100
Bethesda, MD 20814

A computerized list of people working with music, imagery and
creativity with children is being compiled and updated by
ICM West, Box 173, Port Townsend, WA 98368.

A *Children's Imagery* cassette, designed to expand creative development in children ages five to twelve, including a descriptive
pamphlet on using guided imagery in the classroom is available from ICM West, Box 173, Port Townsend, WA 98368.
The cassette was created by Ann McClure and Marilyn
Spafford.

Accelerated Learning

Dr. Georgi Lozanov. *Suggestology.* New York: Gordon and
Breech, 1979.

Dr. Ivan Barzakov. *Optimalearning.* Barzak Educational Institute,
6 Knoll Lane, Suite A-2, Mill Valley, CA 94941.

Charles Schmid, Ph.D., Learning in New Dimensions (LIND),
4245 18th Street, San Francisco, CA 94114.

Sheila Ostrander and Lynn Schroeder. *Superlearning.* New York:
Delacorte, 1979.

RESOURCES AND REFERENCES

On Noise

Acoustical Society of America
335 East 45th Street
New York, NY 10017
212/661-9494

EPA (Environmental Protection Agency)
Office of Air, Noise, and Radiation
401 M Street NW
Washington, D.C. 20460
202/755-2640
The EPA has regional public informational offices. There may be one in your area.

Federal Aviation Administration
Department of Transportation
800 Independence Avenue SW
Washington, D.C. 20591
202/655-4000

National Association of Noise Control Officials (NANCO)
P.O. Box 2618
Fort Walton Beach, FL 32549
904/243-8129

On Hearing Impairment

American Council of Otolaryngology
1101 Vermont Avenue NW
Washington, D.C. 20036
202/293-4607

The American Speech-Language-Hearing Association
10801 Rockville Pike
Rockvile, MD 20852
301/897-5700

American Tinnitus Association
P.O. Box 5
Portland, OR 97207

Auditory Research
P.O. Box 549
Minneapolis, MN 55440
Send for information on audio cassette series.

Better Hearing Institute
1430 K Street NW, Suite 600
Washington, D.C. 20005
202/638-7577

The National Information Center for Quiet
Box 57171
Washington, D.C. 20037

Noise Counseling Program
1909 K Street NW
Washington, D.C. 20049
202/872-4700
   Sponsored by NRTA-AARP, The National Retired Teachers Association, a division of American Association of Retired
Persons.

SHHH (Self Help for Hard of Hearing People, Inc.)
4848 Battery Lane, Suite 100
Bethesda, MD 20814
301/657-2248 (V) and 657-2249 (TTY)
   SHHH is a very personal organization based in the Washington, D.C. metropolitan area whose goal is "making hearing
loss an issue of national concern." SHHH publishes a magazine and a number of self-help programs.

On Music and Therapy

Helen L. Bonny: *Music Rx*. ICM West, P.O. Box 173, Port Townsend, WA 98368. Telephone 206/385-6160 or 385-3743. The basic *Music Rx* package includes five taped music cassettes (eight complete listening programs), one taped voice instruction cassette, and a twelve-page instruction booklet for use in hospitals. Cost: $200.00

Steven Halpern: *Hospital Suite*: long-playing reel-to-reel or cartridge or extended play cassettes.
Sound Attunement Series: Twelve compositions, each lasting an entire side of a cassette, in each of the twelve keys. Especially useful in conjunction with applied kinesiology or massage.
Anti-Frantic Alternative® *Tapes*. Available from Halpern Sounds, 1775 Old County Road #9, Belmont, CA 94002. 800/544-4444.

National Association for Music Therapy: 1133 15th Street NW, Washington, D.C. 20005, 202/429-9440. This Association publishes the monthly *Journal for Music Therapy* and can refer people to schools that offer courses and programs related to music therapy.

References

Bibliography of Noise Publications (1972–1982) U.S. Environmental Protection Agency. Write to:
National Technical Information Service
Department of Commerce
5285 Port Royal Road
Springfield, VA 22161
703/487-4650
Descriptive references to more than three hundred governmental publications.

Borzomenyi and Robbins. *San Diego, California: Case History of a Municipal Noise Control Program.*
EPA Office of Noise Abatement and Control
Washington, D.C.
    1978. EPA #550/9-79-406, NTIS# PB 82-226739.

Shhh: A Journal About Hearing Loss (bimonthly)
    Box 34889
    Bethesda, MD 20817
    Popular-magazine format on self-help for people with hearing loss; magazine comes to all members of Self Help for Hard of Hearing People, Inc. Annual dues; under $10.00

Noise Control Handbook: A Practical Guide in Solving Noise Problems, published by Bruel & Kjaer Instruments, Inc.
    185 Forest Street
    Marlborough, MA 01752
    617/481-7000
    An ideal handbook for those making their first attempt at practical community or industrial noise control; a reference work. 156 pp. Cost: $6.00.

W.D. Keidel, S. Kallert, and M. Korth, *The Physiological Basis of Hearing: A Review.* New York: Thieme-Stratton, 1982. Cost: $25.00.
    Comprehensive and thorough review of auditory physiology.

Maurice H. Miller and Carol A. Silverman, eds. *Occupational Hearing Conservation.* Englewood Cliffs, New Jersey: Prentice-Hall, 1983.
    Contains a tremendous amount of information.

Quiet Communities Program Demonstration: Final Report.
    EPA Office of Noise Abatement and Control
    Washington, D.C. 1982
        EPA #55019-82-411, NTIS# PB 82-220716.

BIBLIOGRAPHY

We'd like to offer these suggestions to those of you who are interested in pursuing the field of sound health in greater depth.

American Speech-Language-Hearing Association. *Noise as a Public Health Problem: Proceedings of the Third International Congress.* ASHA Report #10. Rockville, Maryland: American Speech-Language-Hearing Association.

Anderson, Neil. *Singing Man.* Tiburon, California: H. J. Kramer, 1980.

Andrews, Donald Hatch. *The Symphony of Life.* Lee's Summit, Missouri: Unity Books, 1966.

Auerbach, Stevanne. *The Whole Child. A Sourcebook.* New York: G.P. Putnam's Sons, 1981.

Barr, Frank, M.D. "Melanin" in *Medical Hypotheses.* Vol. 11: 1–140. 1983.

Bentov, Itzhak. *Stalking the Wild Pendulum.* New York: E. P. Dutton, 1977.

Berland, Theodore. *The Fight for Quiet.* Englewood Cliffs, New Jersey: Prentice-Hall, 1970.

Berstein, Mark. *The Rainbow Book.* Berkeley, California: Shambhala, 1975.

Blair, Lawrence. *Rhythms of Vision.* New York: Schocken Books, Inc. 1976.

Bonny, Helen L. *Facilitating GIM Sessions.* Baltimore: Institute for Consciousness and Music, 1978.

Bonny, Helen and Louis Savary. *Music and Your Mind: Listening with a New Consciousness.* New York: Harper & Row, 1973.

Bonny, Helen L. *Music Rx.* Port Townsend, Washington: ICM West, 1983.

Bragdon, Clifford. *Noise Pollution—The Unquiet Crisis.* Philadelphia: University of Pennsylvania Press, 1971.

Bresler, David E., M.D. *Free Yourself From Pain.* New York: Simon & Schuster, 1979.

Brown, Rosemary. *Immortals By My Side.* Chicago: Henry Regnery, 1974.

Cage, John. *A Year from Monday.* Middletown, Connecticut: Wesleyan University Press, 1963.

Callahan, Philip. *Tuning in to Nature: Solar Energy, Infrared Radiation and the Insect Communication System.* New York: Devin-Adair, 1975.

Campbell, Donald. *Introduction to the Musical Brain.* St. Louis, Missouri: Magnamusic-Baton, 1984.

Carmen, Richard. *Positive Solutions to Hearing Loss.* Englewood Cliffs, New Jersey: Prentice-Hall, 1983.

Carmen, Richard. *Our Endangered Hearing.* Emmaus, Pennsylvania: Rodale Press, 1977.

Chase, Mildred. *Just Being at the Piano.* Culver City, California: Peace Press, 1974.

Clark, Linda. *The Ancient Art of Color Therapy.* Old Greenwich, Connecticut: Devon-Adair, 1975.

Clynes, Manfred, ed. *Music, Mind and Brain: The Neuropsychology of Music.* New York: Plenum Press, 1982.

Clynes, Manfred. *Sentics: The Touch of Emotions.* Garden City, New York: Doubleday, 1977.

Cohen, Sheldon. "Sound Effects on Behavior," *Psychology Today.* (October 1981), pp. 38–49.

Cohen, Sheldon. *Behavior, Health, and Environmental Stress.* New York: Plenum, 1982.

Cousins, Norman. *The Anatomy of an Illness.* New York: Norton, 1979.

David, Nada. *Sing With Your Soul.* Clearwater, Florida: Polyphonia, 1979.

Diamond, John, M.D. *Behavioral Kinesiology.* New York: Harper & Row, 1979. (Published in paperback as *Your Body Doesn't Lie.* New York: Warner Books, 1980.)

Diamond, John, M.D. *The Life Energy in Music, Vols. I and II.* New York: Archaeus Press, 1981, 1983.

Don, Frank. *Color Your World.* New York: Warner Destiny Books, 1977.

Eagle, Charles, ed. *Music Therapy Index, Vols. I and II.* An International Interdisciplinary Index to the Literature of the Psychology, Psycho-Physiology, Psychophysics and Sociology of Music. Lawrence, Kansas: National Association for Music Therapy, 1976,1980, 1983.

Frith, Simon. *Sound Effects: Youth, Leisure, and the Politics of Rock and Roll.* New York: Pantheon Books, 1981.

Gallert, Mark. *New Light on Therapeutic Energies*. London: James Clarke & Co., 1966.

Gallwey, W. Timothy. *The Inner Game of Golf*. New York: Random House, 1979.

Gallwey, W. Timothy. *The Inner Game of Tennis*. New York: Bantam Books, 1974.

Feltman, John. "Healing with Light and Sound," *Prevention Magazine*. (Jun 1981), pp. 86–91.

Funk, Joel. "Music and Fourfold Vision," *ReVision*, vol. 6, no. 1 (Spring, 1983), pp. 57–65.

Gutheil, Emil, ed. *Music and Your Emotions*. New York: Liveright, 1952.

Halpern, Steven. *Music Making for Non-Musicians*. Belmont, California: Halpern Sounds, 1984. (Booklet and tape.)

Halpern, Steven. "Some Notes and Thoughts on Spiritual Music," *American Theosophist*. 70 (5) 1982, pp. 116–121.

Halpern, Steven. *Toward a Contemporary Psychology of Music*. San Francisco: Lone Mountain College, 1973. (Master's Thesis.)

Halpern, Steven. *Tuning the Human Instrument*. Belmont, California: Spectrum Research Institute, 1978.

Hamel, Peter Michael. *Through Music to the Self: How to Appreciate and Experience Music Anew*. London: Compton Press, 1976.

Heline, Corrine. *Esoteric Music*. Marina del Rey, California: DeVorss, 1969.

Heline, Corrine. *Healing and Regeneration through Music*. Santa Barbara: New Age Press, 1969.

Herbert, W. "Too Noisy to Think: Infant Learning Lags," *Science News*. Vol. 122:133 (August 28, 1982).

Hill, Stephen and Anna Turner. *Music from the Hearts of Space*. San Francisco:

Hills, Christopher. *Supersensonics: the Science of Radiational Paraphysics*. Boulder Creek, California: University of the Trees Press, 1972.

Holbrooke, B. "Sound Effects: Why Noise Makes You Nervous?" *Mademoiselle*. Vol. 8: 45–6. (July 1982).

Houston, Jean. *Life-Force: The Psycho-Historical Recovery of the Self*. New York: Delacorte, 1980.

Houston, Jean and Robert Masters. *Listening to the Body*. New York: Delacorte, 1978.

Houston, Jean. *The Possible Human*. Los Angeles: J. P. Tarcher, 1982.

Huang, Chung-Liang Al. *Quantum Soup: A Philosophical Entertainment*. New York: Dutton, 1983.

Jenny, Hans. *Cymatics: The Structure and Dynamics of Waves and Vibrations*, Vols. I and II. Basel, Switzerland: Basilius Press, 1967.

Johnston, William. *Silent Music*. New York: Harper & Row, 1974.

Journal of Music Therapy. Washington, D.C.: National Association for Music Therapy.

Kelly, Timothy. *Teach Yourself Singing*. Menlo Park, California: IWP Publishing, 1980.

Key, Wilson Bryan. *Subliminal Seduction*. Englewood Cliffs, New Jersey: Prentice-Hall, 1973.

Keyes, Elizabeth Laurel. *Toning: The Creative Power of the Voice*. Marina del Rey, California: DeVorss, 1978.

Khan, Hazrat Inayat. *Music*. New York: Samuel Weiser, 1962.

Khan, Hazrat Inayat. *The Mysticism of Sound*. New York: Weber, 1979.

Kiedel, W.D., *et al. The Physiological Basis of Hearing: A Review*. New York: Thieme-Stratton, 1982.

Krippner, Stanley. *Galaxies of Life: Acupuncture and the Human Aura*. New York: Macmillan Press, 1973.

Langer, Susan. *Philosophy in a New Key*. New York: Mentor, 1942.

Leonard, George. *The Silent Pulse*. New York: Bantam New Age Books, 1981.

Lingerman, Hal A. *The Healing Energies of Music*. Wheaton, Illinois: Theosophical Publishing House, 1983.

Lipscomb, David M. *Noise: The Unwanted Sounds*. New York: Nelson-Hall Publisher, 1974.

Llaurado, J.G. and A. Sances. *Biologic and Clinical Effects of Low Frequency Magnetic and Radiational Fields*. Springfield, Illinois: Charles Thomas, 1974.

Maleskey, Gale. "Music that Strikes a Healing Chord," *Prevention Magazine*. (October 1983), pp. 57–63.

Mazer, Ellen. "Keep on Hearing Life's High Notes," *Prevention*. (January 1983), pp. 104–112.

McClure, Ann and Marilyn Spafford. *Children's Imagery*. Port Townsend, Washington: ICM West, 1983. (Cassette and Booklet.)

Meek, George. *From Seance to Science*. London: Regency Press, 1973.

Mendelsohn, Robert S., M.D. *Confessions of a Medical Heretic*. New York: Warner Books, 1979.

Miller, Maurice and Carol A. Silverman, eds. *Occupational Hearing Conservation*. Englewood Cliffs, New Jersey: Prentice-Hall, 1983.

Motoyama, Hiroshi. *Theories of the Chakras: Bridge to Higher Consciousness*. New York: Harper & Row, 1973.

Navarra, J. G. *Our Noisy World*. New York: Doubleday, 1969.

Newsweek. "A Healthy Dose of Laughter," (Oct 4, 1982), p. 74. (Includes comments by Dr. William Fry).

Olishefski, Julian and Earl Harford, eds. *Industrial Hearing Conservation in Noise Control*. Chicago: National Safety Council, 1975.

Operation Shhh. Bethesda, Maryland: Self Help for Hard of Hearing People, Inc., 1984.

Ostrander, Sheila and Lynn and Nancy Schroeder. *Super-Learning*. New York: Delacorte, 1979.

Ott, John. *Health and Light: The Effects of Natural and Artificial Light on Man and Other Living Things*. New York: Pocket Books, 1973.

Oyle, Irving, M.D. *The Healing Mind*. Millbrae, California: Celestial Arts, 1975.

Peterson, E. A., *et al.* "Noise Raises Blood Pressure Without Impairing Auditory Sensitivity (rhesus monkeys)," *Science*. 211: 1450–2. (March 27, 1981).

Raloff, J. "Airport Noise Linked with Heart Disease (research by William Meecham and Neil Shaw)," *Science News*. 123:294. (May 7, 1983).

Raloff, Janet. "Occupational Noise—The Subtle Pollutant." *Science News*. vol. 121: 347–350. (May 22, 1982).

Reck, David. *Music of the Whole Earth*. New York: Charles Scribner's Sons, 1977.

Retallack, Dorothy. *The Sound of Music and Plants*. Santa Monica, California: DeVorss, 195.

Rodan, Gideon A., Elizabeth Bourret, and Louis Norton. *Science*. 199: 690–692. (1977). (Report on R. F. Becker's research).

Roederer, Juan. "Music Perceptions and Basic Functions of the Human Brain," in Manfred Clynes, ed. *Music, Mind and Brain*. New York: Plenum Press, 1982.

Royster, J. D. and L. Royster. "STS: How to Gauge the Noise Problem (significant threshold shifts)" *Science News*. 123: 21. (January 8, 1983).

Rudhyar, Dane. *The Magic of Tone and the Art of Music*. Boulder, Colorado: Shambala, 1982.

Savary, Louis M. and Patricia H. Berne. *Prayerways*. New York: Harper & Row, 1980.

Schafer, R. Murray. *The Tuning of the World*. New York: Knopf, 1977.

Scott, Cyrill. *Music: Its Secret Influence Through the Ages*. London: Theosophical Publishing House, 1937.

Seashore, Carl. *Psychology of Music*. New York: McGraw-Hill, 1938.

Seebohm, Caroline. "In Search of a Quieter Life," *House & Garden*. (February, 1979), p. 104.

Shealy, C. and M. V. Norman. *The Pain Game*. Millbrae, California: Celestial Arts, 1976.

Sheldrake, Rupert. *A New Science of Life*. Los Angeles, California: Tarcher, 1981.

Shhh: A Journal About Hearing Loss. Box 34889, Bethesda, Maryland 20817.

Slonimsky, Nicolas. *Lexicon of Musical Invective: Critical Assaults on Composers since Beethoven's Time*. St. Louis: Washington University Press, 1953.

Stebbin, Lionel. *Music: Its Occult Basis and Healing Value*. London: New Knowledge Books, 1972.

Stevens, S. S. and F. Warshofsdy. *Sound and Hearing*. New York: Time-Life Books, 1965.

Stone, Andy. *Song of the Kingdom*. New York: Doubleday, 1979.

Sullivan, J. W. M. *Beethoven: His Spiritual Development*. New York: Knopf, 1964.

Simoneton, Andre. "Brain Mind Bulletin." Box 42211, Los Angeles, California 90042.

Taylor, I. A. and F. Paperte. "Current Theory and Research in the Effects of Music on Behavior," *Journal of Aesthetics*. Vol. 17: 251–258. (1958).

Taylor, Byrd and Peter Parnall. *The Other Way to Listen*. New York: Scribners, 1978.

Teilhard de Chardin, Pierre. *The Divine Milieu*. New York: Harper & Row, 1961.

Tompkins, Peter, and Christopher Bird. *The Secret Life of Plants*. New York: Harper & Row, 1972.

Underwood, Lee. *World Music and Inner Transformation*. Milwaukee: Narada, 1984.

United States Environmental Protection Agency. *Noise Around Our Home*. Washington, D.C.: U.S. EPA, March 1980. (Booklet.)

Watkins, Mary M. *Waking Dreams*. New York: Harper & Row, 1977. (Excellent survey of Jung's approach to imagination and symbolism).

White, D. "Britain Gets Noisier," *Psychology Today*. Vol. 15:45–46. (October 1981.)

Whone, Herbert. *The Hidden Face of Music*. New York: The Garden Studio, 1978.

Willcott, J. F. and S-M. Lu. "Noise-Induced Hearing Loss Can Alter Neural Coding and Increase Excitability in the Central Nervous System," *Science*. Vol. 216:1331–2. (June 18, 1982.)

Winternitz, Emanuel. *Musical Instruments and Their Symbolism in Western Art*. New Haven, Connecticut: Yale University Press, 1979.

Zuckerkandl, Victor. *Sound and Symbol: Music and the External World*. Princeton: Princeton University Press, 1969.

Tapes

Budzynski, Thomas. *Futurehealth*. 2150 Bristol Pike, Bensalem, PA. Free catalog features Subliminal Programming tapes and Bio-Q biofeedback rings.

Diamond, John, M.D. *Biological Harmonics*. Institutes for the Enhancement of Life Energy and Creativity. P.O. Drawer 37, Valley Cottage, NY 10989. Life energy enhancing music tapes.

Halpern, Steven. *The Anti-Frantic Alternative® Series*. Uniquely beautiful music for relaxation or pure listening pleasure. Sixteen titles, including *Spectrum Suite, Eventide*, and *Soft Focus*.
Soundwave 2000®. Anti-Frantic® music plus Harmonic Affirmations®, including *The Joy of Learning*.
Write Halpern Sounds, 1775 Old County Road, #9, Belmont, California 94002. For a free catalog, call (415) 592-4900 or (800) 544-4444.

Konicov, Barrie. *Potentials Unlimited*. 4808 H Broadmoor, S.E., Grand Rapids, MI 49508. Over 150 titles in free catalog.

Miller, Emmett, M.D. *Source Cassette Learning Systems*. 945 Evelyn Street, Menlo Park, CA 94025. Many people relax as soon as they hear his extraordinary voice. Free catalog, featuring Threshold Affirmations®.

Rossman, Martin. *Insight Training*. 1775 Old County Road #10, Belmont, CA 94002. Free Catalog.

Savary, Louis M. and Steven Halpern. *A Centering Meditation* (on the Lord's Prayer). Credence Cassettes, Box 281, Kansas City, MO. 1975.

Sutphen, Richard. *Self-Help Update*. Valley of the Sun Publishing Co., Box 2010, Malibu, CA 90265. Over 200 titles in their free catalog.